Henry Tuckley

In Sunny France

Present-day life in the French republic

Henry Tuckley

In Sunny France
Present-day life in the French republic

ISBN/EAN: 9783744743266

Printed in Europe, USA, Canada, Australia, Japan

Cover: Foto ©ninafisch / pixelio.de

More available books at **www.hansebooks.com**

IN SUNNY FRANCE

PRESENT-DAY LIFE IN THE FRENCH REPUBLIC

BY

HENRY TUCKLEY

AUTHOR OF "UNDER THE QUEEN," "QUESTIONS OF THE HEART,"
"MASSES AND CLASSES," "THE LATTER-DAY EDEN," ETC.

CINCINNATI: CRANSTON & CURTS
NEW YORK: HUNT & EATON
1894

PREFATORY NOTE.

THESE sketches of folks and things in France, the product of considerable observation and study, are humbly offered to those readers who may wish to inform or refresh themselves in a general and pleasant way upon the most interesting phases of French life without devoting much time to the subject; and the author is joined by the devoted companion of his journeys and labors in specially dedicating this little work, as a token of affectionate regard and in memory of much delightful fellowship, to Mr. and Mrs. Frank H. Maynard, of Providence, Rhode Island, dear friends of ours, who happily combine, with a rare love of home and native land, a great liking for travel, and an intelligent appreciation of life and affairs in the nations of Europe.

HENRY TUCKLEY.

2133215

IN SUNNY FRANCE.

TABLE OF CONTENTS.

I.

PARIS AND LONDON.

First Impressions—A Tale of Two Cities—How they differ from Each Other—"London for Commerce; Paris for Gayety"—Proverbial Notions confirmed—The Struggle of Life—A Pathetic Caution—Dynamite and the Commune—The Masses in London and Paris: A Contrast—Drunkenness in the Two Cities—Parisian Cafés—Parisian Architecture: A Complaint—Another Contrast with London—Architectural Monotony—"Such a getting Up-stairs"—Features in which Paris is Unrivaled—The View from Place de la Concorde—Paris by Gaslight—Bewildering Mazes—The Parisian Cabman—His Loud Ways and Low Charges—An Instance of Good Horse-sense—Parisian Policemen—The Principal Thing in Paris—French Poodles—Passing View of Parisian Swells—Ladies and Babies—Some Paris Fashions, . . Pages 20–30.

II.

AMERICANS IN PARIS.

American Students at the French Capital—Lessons in Language—What they cost—Pupils in Music—Advantages of Foreign Study—What the Students say—Spending a Fortune to make One—A Case in Point—Paris as an Art Center—French Generosity—Novitiates of the Brush and Easel—Fine Opportunities at Small Cost—The Ecole des Beaux Arts—Dining the Professors—Women in the Art Studio—Gallantry that pays—The Social Life of Art Students—How the Girls are cared for—A Place of

Sweetness and Light—American "At Homes" in Paris
—A Wholesome Warning—Parisian Pitfalls—Gifted American Boys—Great Painters in Embryo—Roughing it in Paris—American Students and the American Minister
—A Tell-tale Titter—The American Art Students' Club—
The Bright Aspects of Student Life—Moral Safeguards.

Pages 31-39.

III.

ON THE BOULEVARDS.

Mementos of Louis XIV—The Paris of the Past—Landmarks of a Great City's Growth—An Interesting Walk—
The Madeleine: Its Significant History—The Portes St. Denis and St. Martin—Sanguinary Scenes of the Last Commune—View from the Place de l'Opera—An Instance of Parisian Enterprise—Rue de la Paix and Column Vendôme—Gruesome Reminders of Bloody Events—
Something Distinctively Parisian—Fragrance Galore—A Paris Mystery—Masks and Faces—Parisian Shops—
Captivating Window Displays—Paris Fashions in Dressed Meat—Sidewalk Looking-glasses—A Weakness of Well-dressed Frenchmen—Parisian Styles in Bill-posting—
Something Less Commendable—America on the Boulevards—From Daylight to Dark—A Change of Scene.

Pages 40-48.

IV.

THE POOR OF PARIS.

Transformation in a Paris Ball-room—A Mothers' Meeting, and the Contrasts it suggested—A Reminder of Pre-revolutionary Days—Life among the Lowly—Sad Lack of Home Comforts—A Feature of Parisian Markets—
Observations in "Old Paris"—Tenements which were formerly Palaces—Narrow Streets and Lofty Stairways—
Poverty in the World's Largest Cities—An Entertaining Talk—Good Traits of Paris Work-people—Where the Communists come from—A Paris Workman's Apartments—Indications of Taste and Thrift—Another Pa-

risian Interior—Love laughing at Poverty—Pleasantly imposed upon—A Novel Argument for Matrimony—The French Marriage Laws—Severe Strictures from an Intelligent Source—Two Illustrative Instances—The Juvenile Contingent of "Old Paris"—A Converted Absinthe-drinker, ... Pages 49-59.

V.

PARIS AND ITS SUBURBS.

Fortifications of the French Capital—A Tribute from German Officialism—The Touch of Nature which makes Frenchmen Akin to Americans—A New Title to Greatness—Present Uses of the Gates of Paris—Troublesome Toll-collectors—The Tax on Meat and Liquors—Ingenious Smugglers—Spirits in Coffins—Another Instance of French Thrift—The Suburbs of Paris—The Contrast they present to the City Itself—Paris Superior to France—Parisian Railways—Chemin de fer de Ceinture and Chemin de fer de Grande Ceinture—Instances of Parisian Backwardness—Trams and Busses—Advantages of the Ticket System—A Familiar Sign—How it misled an Enterprising Irishman—The Parisian Style in Horse-hair—Gray Horses and Strawberry Blondes—Striking Contradiction of an Old Proverb—Parisian Cabs—Further Examples of Parisian Style, ... Pages 60-68.

VI.

THE STREETS OF PARIS.

A Perennial Source of Pleasure—Paris as an Example to Other Cities—A Source of Annoyance—Paris Flats—The Typical Parisian House—Distressing Uniformity—Street Nomenclature — A Present-day Parisian Mania — For Changed Times, Different Names—How the Saints are honored in a Gay City—Honors to Americans—Rue Washington and Rue Lincoln—The American Colony in Paris: Its Dimensions and Beautiful Location—American Churches—Two Enterprising Clergymen—Large

Plans and Good Work—Unique Street Effects—Rue de Rivoli and Palais Royal—Other Characteristic Localities Boulevards Voltaire, Magenta, Sevastopol, and Strasbourg—Entrancing Vistas—Avenue de la Grande Armée How Paris still honors Germany—A Boat-ride on the Seine—The Wonderful Panorama it reveals.
Pages 69-76.

VII.

SOME PARISIAN NOVELTIES.

The World's Shopping Center—Of Interest to Both Sexes—The Bon Marché—The Novelty of Fixed Prices—Customers their own Cash-boys—A Fortune by a Fad—A Peddler's Pack and its Marvelous Expansion—A Tale worth telling—Bounties and Pensions for Faithful Employees—Philanthropic Recognition of a Great City's Confidence and Patronage—A Novelty in Hospitals—The Famous Pasteur Institute—Encouraging Progress—From Hospital to Church—The Shrine of Our Lady of Victory—A Favorite Resort of Ex-Empress Eugenie—A Maze of Lighted Candles—What it signifies—Memorials of Answered Prayers—Gratitude in Marble—By Rail to Ivry—Horse-flesh as an Article of Food—Signs of Mercantile Honesty—A Rag-pickers' Cité—Wages of Factory Hands—"What's in a Name?"—A Novelty in Tenements—Cité Jeanne d'Arc, ... Pages 77-86.

VIII.

BENEATH THE SURFACE IN PARIS.

The Topic qualified and explained—Looking for the Good in a Great City—Paris and London compared morally—Heroic Reformers—Young Men in Paris—A Great Awakening—An Importation from the United States—The Christian Endeavor Movement—A Thriving Y. M. C. A.—A Philanthropic American—Student life in Paris—Dark Features and Bright—A Visit to the Latin Quarter—Moral and Religious Activity—A Counter-attraction to the Café—America still to' the Front—The McAll Mission—How it is supported—An Evangel to the Poor—Unreasonable Expectations—A New Departure in Mission-work—Testimony of a French Official—Eloquent Statistics, ... Pages 87–95.

IX.
THE FRENCH REPUBLIC.

Governmental Kinship between France and the United States—Sisters or Cousins: Which?—Points of Resemblance—The Electoral Franchise—A Study in Governmental Anatomy—Points of Divergence—The French Republic and the British Monarchy—The French Cabinet—Privileges of Ministers—Chief Occupation of President Carnot—Presidential Resignations—The French Constitution: Is it a Misfit?—The Veto Power—Safeguards against Royalist Plotters—Mode of electing a President—Another Divergence from American Methods—Where the Two Republics are Significantly Alike—Great Names at a Discount—Changes in the Ministry: Why so Frequent?—Political Factions—The Dread of Despots—Salary and Duties of the French President—Republican Magnificence — Presidential Patronage — A Legacy from the Empire, ... Pages 96–104.

X.
THE LEGISLATIVE SYSTEM.

A Glance at the Past—Monarchists and the Republic—The Two-chamber Plan: How it originated and how it works—The Chamber of Deputies—Characteristic Traits and Tendencies—Need of a Constitutional Check—The Average French Deputy—Fisticuffs and Dueling—The French Senate—Qualifications of Senators—How they are elected—Life Senators—A Recent Constitutional Reform—Relative Powers of the Two Chambers—Custom encroaching on Law—Small Salaries and Great Temptations—Organizing for Business—Taking a Vote—An Imposing Formality—Political Promises: A New Way to get rid of them—A Suggestion for American Congressmen—Legislative Independence—Greatest Need of the French Republic—Joint Sessions at Versailles—The Palais de Luxembourg: Its History and Present Use—The Palais Bourbon as a Legislative Chamber.

Pages 105-113.

XI.
COURTS OF LAW IN FRANCE.

Imprints of a Great Genius—The Code Napoleon: Its Origin, Scope, and Potency—Appointments to the Judiciary—The Ministry of Justice—The Supreme Court—Public Officials in France—Salaries of Judges—A Striking Contrast with England—Justice at Cheap Rates—The Other Side—Courts of the First Instance—Courts of Appeal—A Peculiar Feature of French Courts—The Parquet—Things to boast of—Judges vs. Juries—Why the Former are preferred—Light on a Vexed Problem—Some Interesting Statistics—Extreme Sentimentality of the French Juryman—"Mitigating Circumstances"—A Weeping Court—Peculiarities of French Judges—Hostility toward the Accused—Judicial Dignity—At the Palais de Justice—A Sacred Reminder—Court-room Habitués—Justice for the Poor—Other Commendable Features.

Pages 114-122.

XII.
THE FRENCH PRESS.

The Panama Revelations—Queer Newspaper Methods—An Open Claimant for Bribes—Astonishing Immunity from Punishment—Newspaper Influence for Sale—Advertisements in Editorials—Attitude of the Government—A Well-known Secret—Payments for Puffs—General Remarks on French Newspapers—One Sense in which Paris is France—The French Press judged by American Ideals—Classification of Parisian Newspapers—Enterprise and Freshness—A Striking Deficiency—Comparison with English Newspapers—Controlling Principles—"Like Public, like Press"—Parisian Tastes and how they are met—

The Naked Truth and the Nude in Art—Publication of Divorce Proceedings— Laudable Restrictions — Another Comparison with England—The Staples of French Newspaper-reading— Personal Responsibility of Editors—Farcical Dueling—A New-found Freedom—The French Reporter, ... Pages 123-131.

XIII.
THE FRENCH PEASANTRY.

Popular Suppositions—A Necessary Correction—Extensive Subdivision of Land—How it originated—A Legacy from the Distant Past—Facts and Figures examined—Farming under Difficulties—Comparison of Results from Large Holdings and Small—The Peasant Proprietor: His Condition Materially—The French Peasant in Contrast with the English—Recent Improvements—Jacques Bonhomme and Honest Hodge—Wages of French Farm-hands—Peasant Contentment—The French Peasant as a Political Force—Why he changes Sides so easily—Depopulation of the Rural Districts—A Comparison with Germany—The Drift toward City Life—The Peasant as a Renter—Peasant Organizations for Mutual Help—An All-round Glance at Peasant Life, ... Pages 132-140.

XIV.
FRENCH HOME-LIFE.

Significant Limitations of the French Language—The French Home in its Material Aspects—"Most at Home when not at Home"—The Formalities of Family Life—The Patriarchal Principle—A Delightful Experience—Honors to Old Age—Proverbial Love of Mother—The Family Feeling: A Far-reaching Sentiment—Pathetic Memorials in French Cemeteries — Unique Funeral Cards — The French Home in its Numerical Aspects—A National Reproach—Relative Growth of Population in France, England, and Germany—Two Instructive Allusions—Thrift degenerating into Sordidness—Governmental Bounties—

Nurses and Babies again—Other Interesting Family Matters—Growing Girlhood: How it is guarded The French Chaperon—Strictures from an Enlightened Frenchman—French Hospitality — Home-life of the Peasantry — Woman's Rights—Some Peculiar Laws, . . Pages 141–151.

XV.
THE EDUCATIONAL SYSTEM.

Progress under the Republic—French Education classified—Striking Instances of Development—Public Lycées for Girls—Secondary Education—What it embraces and what it costs—Generous Distribution of Scholarships—State Control of Degrees—Church and State in Fierce Conflict—The Government Triumphant—Qualifications of Teachers—Sweeping Reforms—The Teaching of Religion—Sensible Attitude of the French Government—Higher Education—The University of France—Paris as an Educational Center—The Catholics and the University—Protestant Faculties of Theology—Discipline in Lycées and Colleges—Strict Surveillance of Pupils—Effeminate Boys and Demure Girls—A System of Seclusion and Repression—Hard Life of the French School Miss—Women and University Training—The Primary Schools—Laws governing them—Separation of the Sexes—Compulsory Attendance and how enforced—The School and the Flag—An Encouraging Outlook, . . . Pages 152–161.

XVI.
MARRIAGE CUSTOMS.

The Preliminaries of Wedlock—Delightful Experiences ruthlessly dispensed with—Popping the Question—How it is *not* done in France—Love-making under Difficulties—Single Blessedness in France—Commonness of Celibacy—"The Matrimonial Market"—A Mania for Dowries—The Luckless Lot of a Girl without a *Dot*—A Plausible Explanation — Customs which stimulate Thrift—The Dowry after Wedlock—Some Distressing Results—Candidates for Matrimony: How they proceed—A Matter of Business—Premature Betrothals—A Schedule of Allowable Familiarities—An Interesting Query—Love laughing at Custom—Marriage and the Civil Law—From the Mayor's Office to Church—The Wedding Ceremony and the Collection-box, ... Pages 162-170.

XVII.

MATTERS OF TASTE.

The French as Conquerors—An Enviable Monopoly—Fancy exceeded by Reality—Living to eat—New Use of an Old Simile—A Deceiving Meal Schedule—A French Assault on the Dinner-table—A Charge of Gourmandism—The Opinion of a Friendly Critic—The French Chef in his Element—Some French Delicacies—The Catch-all of the French Kitchen—Public Drinking in France—Café Life—Favorite Pastime of the Average Parisian—The Popular Love of Wine—Women as Wine-drinkers—French and English Women in Contrast—Immoderate Moderation—A Change for the Worse—The Consumption of Alcohol in Different Provinces—A Diminished Wine-crop—Alarming Spread of Drunkenness—Police Court Statistics—Absinthe and Eau de Vie—Increased Indulgence and Deadly Consequences—Testimony from a Competent Witness—A Gratifying Discovery—The Blue Cross Temperance Society—Statistics of Progress, . . Pages 171-183.

XVIII.

CHURCH AND STATE.

Roman Catholicism and the French Government—A Famous Encyclical—Attitude of the Church toward the Republic—The Recent Change—President Carnot and Leo XIII—Implacable Nobles—The Pope and Panama—Limitations of a Papal Edict—What Protestants say—A Question of Motives—Self-inflicted Martyrdom—Expulsion of the Jesuits—Confiscation of Church Lands—Eng-

lish Critics worthily answered—Crosses on Cemetery Gates—Suppression of Unauthorized Brotherhoods—The Republic fighting for its Life—Suicide as Evidence of Guilt—Catholicism and the Public Schools—Equal Rights granted, but Ascendency denied—Attitude of the Republic toward Religion—State Aid for Catholics, Protestants, Jews, and Mohammedans—State Control: How exercised—Voting Supplies—Glance at the Annual Budget—A Significant Situation—Where the Catholic Church has failed—The Church and the Peasantry—Prevalent Skepticism—Opposition of the Church to Wholesome Reforms—What Frenchmen themselves say.
Pages 184–193.

XIX.

French Protestantism.

Numerical Strength of French Protestantism—How it is divided—Protestantism and State Aid—Religious Equality under the Republic—An Outspoken Clergyman—Influence wielded by French Protestantism—Protestants in Public Office—Illustrious Protestant Names—Relative Influence of Protestants and Catholics—Views of an American Priest—A Tribute from President Carnot—Protestants and the Republic—Pathetic Revelations—A Bloody History recalled—Where Protestantism is Supreme—Department of the Gard—Some Striking Facts—Protestantism at its Best—Protestantism under Napoleon III—Protestant Newspapers—Protestant Losses in 1871—Feeling of French Protestants toward Germany—The Question of Disestablishment—Threats of the Radicals—The Calm View of a French Pastor—The Peasant as a Possible Revolutionist—After Disestablishment, What?—A Beautiful Ideal—Preparing for the Worst—Evangelicalism and Rationalism—A Glance at the Past—Present Conditions—Open Doors of Opportunity—An Active Campaign—Gains from Catholicism—An Appeal for Help, ... Pages 194–205.

XX.

THE CONTINENTAL SUNDAY.

A Live Topic in Europe—Opposite Trends in Europe and America—A New Putting of the Sunday Question—Mistaken Notions corrected—Americans Abroad—Gratifying Advances—A Glance at Berlin—Professor von Treitschke on the American Sunday—German Opposition to Sunday Labor—Stringent Laws—The Present Situation—Sabbath-keeping in the German Capital—A Working class Movement—Wholesome Sop for Social Democrats—On to Paris—Growth of Sentiment in the French Capital—A Sunday Observance Society—Two Eloquent Reformers: Jules Simon and Leon Say—A Statement of Principles—Some Practical Results—Paris on Sunday—Signs of Progress—A Scandalous Fallacy—Reforms in the Railway and Postal Service—Paris as a Rival of Sabbath-keeping London—The Sunday Question and the Churches, ... Pages 206-214.

XXI.

FRENCH HOLIDAY-MAKING.

The French as Extremists—Where the Catholic Church is Still Supreme—Bank Holidays in France—Feast of the Assumption: How it is observed—All Saints and All Souls—At Pere la Chaise—The French Decoration-day—Merry Christmas—Realistic Art in the Churches—The Midnight Mass—A Tax on Solemnity—Christmas at St. Roche's—Santa Claus at a Discount—French Anglomaniacs — New Year's in France — Expositions des Etrennes—Costly Bonbons and Ravishing Dolls—Transformation of the Great Boulevards—Baraques du Jour de l'an—The Rage of the Hour—New Year's Gifts—The Exchange of Visiting-cards—Busy Times in Postal Circles—The Concierge and his Exactions—Remembering the Poor—New Year's at the Palais Elysée—Turkey and Truffles—The New Year and the Peasantry.

Pages 215-223

XXII.
POVERTY AND WEALTH.

Material Condition of the French Nation—Indications of Abounding Wealth—Number of House-owners and Landed Proprietors—Where France stands Unrivaled—Solvency of the French Government—Proofs of Popular Confidence—The Country Folk on Dividend-day—An Inspiring Procession—The Eiffel Tower—French Engineering paralleled by French Thrift—The Postal Savings Bank: Its Wonderful Development and Present Status—Figures from an Unbiased Source—Report of the United States Consul at Bordeaux—Material Growth in Twenty Years—The Reverse Side—A Mammoth National Debt—How it has increased under the Republic—Comparison of France with Other Nations—What will the End be?—A Predicted Collapse—Financial Genius which inspires Hope—The Problem of Poverty—France and England again—The Assistance Publique—How it is supported and administered—Novel Methods of Taxation.
Pages 224-231.

XXIII.
THE WAR-CLOUD.

Military Affairs in Europe—Explanation of the Periodical War-scare—A Question of Environment—Difference between France and the United States—Significant Figures—A Century's Tribute to European Battle-fields—"They all do it"—Preparations for War: Are they a Guaranty of Peace?—Superficial Safeguards—France the Arbiter of its Own Fortunes—Restiveness of the French under Defeat—National Feeling against Germany—French Sentiment and French Dismemberment—The Ironical Congratulations of a Russian Diplomat—An Unfinished Inscription—A Rhetorical Invasion—Count von Caprivi puts his Foot in it—The French View of a Famous Speech—Strange Bedfellows—The Republican Lamb and the Russian Bear—France as a Military Camp—Physique of French Soldiers—The Next War and its Probable Effects on the Republic, ... Pages 232-240.

XXIV.

CONTRASTS AND CONCLUSIONS.

A Bundle of Contradictions—The Most Interesting Nationality in Europe—Lights and Shadows in French Life—Craving what they Scorn—Striking Religious Traits—How Extremes meet in French Femininity—In the Social Realm—Household Attachments and Café-life—Startling Divorce Statistics—French Politeness and its Opposite—Kissing and Dueling—"Only One Paris"—City Gayety and Country Dullness—The Worship and Oppression of Womanhood—Serious Defects in French Law—A Dark Social Blot—Where Sentiment and Practice are at Variance—In the Political Realm—A Loud Call for Charity—Aristocracy vs. Democracy—Sham Nobles—The Legion of Honor—Two Contradictory Occurrences—The Love of Glory—Great Leaders needed—Liberty and Equality with Reservations—Where Danger lurks.

Pages 241-249.

IN SUNNY FRANCE.

I.

PARIS AND LONDON.

IN comparing Paris with London the opinion grows upon us that the capital of the British Empire is far in the lead of the French capital in the things which tend to security and national greatness. To speak generally, London is the business city and Paris the pleasure city of the world. To spend money, one should certainly come to the city on the Seine; but if a center for safe investments were desired, preference would surely be given to the city on the Thames. There is nothing in Paris that inspires such confidence as one feels in looking at the Bank of England, and no doubt the Parisians are thankful not to have in their midst a pile so unsightly. They would hardly accept it for the money it contains. Far more to Parisian taste is the Arc de Triomphe, with its vast circular Place de l'Etoile, and the round dozen of magnificent avenues which slope therefrom into all parts of this wonderful city. The English capital has nothing to compare to this; and, on the other hand, Paris has nothing so grand in the way of churches—nothing that is so large, or that invites so much reverence—as either St. Paul's or Westminster Abbey. The Palais Bourbon, in which the French laws are made, is insignificant when you recall the British Houses of Parliament.

In this city the biggest tides of traffic are found, not, as in London, where the representatives of a mighty commerce congregate, but on avenues where fashion disports itself, like the Avenue de Champs Elysées, the Boulevard des Italiens, and that still wider and grander thoroughfare leading to the Bois de Bologne. And all these things are in keeping with the proverbial notion of the two places: London for commerce, Paris for gayety; London as the capital of a nation with a sure future, Paris as the city which—regardless of what the future may bring—is bent on having a good time right now.

In many things, of course, the two largest cities in the world are alike. Paris, though it is so gay, has a darker side; and if one had time to hunt up its miseries, we should probably find that the struggle of life is just as real and quite as hard for the masses, notwithstanding their bright surroundings, as that which goes on under the gloomy skies and amid the somber buildings of the big city across the channel. Knowing of our purpose to write, an intelligent Parisian lady said to us: "Whatever you do, don't say we are all happy." No, the people are not all happy. There is pinching want here as elsewhere, and it would perhaps be difficult to find any city in which the lower classes are so little contented. It is the knowledge of this that makes thoughtful Frenchmen shrug their shoulders with such a manifest spasm of apprehension when you ask as to the likelihood of another rising of the Commune. It is this which makes Paris so panicky after an explosion of dynamite, and which renders it almost certain that two such explosions in quick succession would shake out of their seats, so to speak, any existing Ministry.

But whether they are better off or not, and spite of the mischief they may again cause, the lower classes of Paris certainly present a more tidy appearance than the same classes in London, and in their out-door life they seem to be more civil and better behaved. It is seldom you see rags and tatters; and to find here such besotted and brutal-looking creatures as you can see all the time on the streets of London, you would surely have to search the slums with that special object in view, and even then you might look in vain. There is more general drinking than in London, but far less drunkenness. The cafés are numerous enough and sufficiently obtrusive, as every visitor well knows, but they are hardly so vicious-looking as the public houses in the world's metropolis. Perhaps their very openness is a means of restraint. Certainly they turn out inebriates at a less rapid rate, and their victims, moreover, are of a type much less repulsive.

After a month or so amid the unvarying stretches of high stone dwellings, all built upon the same general plan and nearly all seeming to be adorned still with the dew and brightness of their youth, the visitor grows weary of this architectural monotony. One can not help wondering why, in this city of art, this particular department of art should have had so little variety infused into it. London is much blacker than Paris, and some of its buildings are hideous monstrosities, but in the charm which diversity gives, it far excels its French rival. No one would suspect London of being a city without a past, for its hoary history is proclaimed wherever you go by frowning, time-worn edifices, which speak unmistakably of ages long gone, and of the gradual progress through those ages of the arts and forces by which great centers of life are built up. Paris has some such memorials as these; but the impression upon the casual visitor must be that it is a city of to-day, quite too new to be venerable, and built on quite too uniform a plan to challenge unqualified admiration. It is beautiful, but one grows tired of seeing so much beauty cast in the same pattern. The American visitor will hardly sympathize with that Londoner whose chief complaint about Paris was, that its high buildings were unfavorable for such a display of chimney-tops as he had been used to at home. But he will surely wish that the houses about him were not *all* so high; and after a little experience in getting to fifth and sixth floors, with elevators as few and far between as angels' visits, his feelings on this subject will become quite too full for utterance.

For long vistas, with trees of uniform height, and stately buildings whose white fronts gleam in the sunlight, and for such effects as one can see in the Place de la Concorde, with the Louvre behind, the mighty Arc de Triomphe looming up in front, the Madeleine to your right, and the gilded dome 'neath which the great Bonaparte rests on the other side of the Seine—the Eiffel Tower also being near enough to be seen to good advantage,—for such things as these, Paris has no equal nor rival. The Circuses at which the thoroughfares of London converge are as mere bagatelle pockets in contrast with the grand *Places* abounding in Paris. The only American city which gives substantial promise of ever competing with the capital of France in broad avenues and magnificent distances is the city of Washington. After night Paris, in the scene of light and change it presents, is like fairyland. To look at the long rows of street-lamps, so much nearer together than in other cities, which, in many places, owing to the length of the streets and boulevards, stretch their lines of beauty so far away from you that the two opposite sides seem at the farther end to come together, and finally to lose themselves in the midst of the clustering lights of some vast circular *Place*—to see a sight like this, as you can a dozen times over in Paris, is simply enchanting. If this city is beautiful by daylight, she is dazzling and almost bewildering by night; and to feel this, one need not have the least share in the mad whirl of life which goes on. You need only take a cab, or view the scene from the top of an omnibus.

Which reminds us, by the way, that Paris and London differ materially in their vehicular service. The London "hansom" is conspicuous here by its rarity. The cabs you find in Paris are four-wheelers, and this difference makes a decided change in the aspect of the streets. One would think that to put the driver immediately behind the horse, instead of perching him on a box behind and above his fare, would conduce to better driving, and hence to the greater security of those having to dodge these vehicles in crossing the streets; but it does n't, by any means. The Parisian cabby drives with a loose rein, and with a very lax regard for the rights of the general public. His heavy shoes, almost like clogs, his shiny hat, painted so as to have a remote resemblance to a genuine silk, and the decided *penchant* he shows for flourishing and cracking his whip,—make him altogether a louder and more disagreeable type than the same species in London. But he charges you very moderately. For thirty cents, with the inevitable fee added, he will take you any distance within the city, providing the journey is not broken. This is the uniform charge. In London you have a slight advantage if your ride is within the mile, but one seldom wants a cab for so short a distance as that; and in Paris you can ride four, five, or even six miles for less than the ordinary rate of a two-mile ride in the metropolis of Great Britain.

By the hour, the cab fare is forty cents. This is extremely moderate; and so also, under this system of hiring, will be the rate of your progress through the Parisian streets. The cab horses here are altogether inferior to those of London. However slow the English themselves may be, they like their horses to make good time; and the London cabman is no exception to this rule. Here, it is the people who are fast; the horses—certainly the cab horses—are very slow. They are slow enough under any circumstances; but it is a proverb with all visitors that if, in making a bargain with cabby, you say, "By the hour," his horse is sure to understand, whether you speak in French or English. We have heard of one man who distinguished himself and obtained several medals by stopping runaway cab-horses. He seemed to know just what to do, and when his secret transpired, it turned out that he checked the mad career of these fiery steeds simply by shouting, as he pulled at the bridle, "By the hour!" After that, the gallop degenerated into a walk from sheer force of habit.

From the ponderous, clumsy-looking policemen of London to the *petit* guardian of the peace in Paris, the change is quite welcome to the eye, although we can not help thinking that the former looks the more business-like of the two. Instead of a club, the Frenchman has a sword dangling from his belt. This, with his high-legged boots, with the cap or cockade he wears, and with the cape, having a hood attached to it, which hangs loosely from his shoulders, gives him more the appearance of a military man out for a saunter, than of one whose presence should be a terror to misdemeanants. But he is very nice to look at, and that seems to be the principal thing in Paris. Everything here appeals to the eye. Even the dogs must be pretty, and many of them are very pretty indeed. The English pug is eschewed as a companion for French ladies—partly, no doubt, because he is English, and partly because he is so outrageously repulsive. The fashion in canines runs to French poodles—a fuzzy, innocent sort of dog; and it is all the style to have part of the fuzz shaved off—the hinder part,—a fancy which, besides adding to the novelty of the dog's appearance, keeps in good circumstances, it is said, quite a number of people who are known professionally as dog-barbers.

The fashions in masculine attire are not so uniform here as in London. In silk hats, one sees all sorts of shapes, and the strangest shapes seem to be most in vogue. The aim of the Parisian swell seems to be, not to conform perfectly to any set code, but rather to defy the codes, and get himself up as picturesquely as possible. Paris does not smoke so much as London, either from its chimney-tops or from beneath its top hats. Parisian ladies have better complexions than the English, and better forms; but in sitting in judgment upon such matters as these, one has to remember that Paris is more a city of art than London is. We have also observed that Parisian women carry themselves with more grace when walking than the English; and as this is a matter which can have no connection with toilet mysteries, we need not hesitate in saying which of the two styles we prefer.

Babies are less numerous here than in London, but those you see are remarkably pretty. So are the nurses who carry them—at least, in their style of dress. They wear, in the autumn, long, circular cloaks, and from their dainty silk caps long streamers of some fashionable shade of ribbon extend the whole length of their attire. Usually the mother is near, and we have noticed many instances in which the shade of ribbon worn by the nurse has some match in the bonnet of this Parisian dame. If not in the bonnet, then you may look for a match at the waist in the form of a sash, or perhaps in the shade of the proud mamma's bodice. Talk of fashion, you have to be in Paris to know fully what it means, and the excesses to which it may run! Fancy these fascinating creatures trimming their petticoats in strict conformity with the style and shade of the hats they may happen to wear! But many of them do this, and it seems to be the fashion for well-dressed women to have the bottoms of their petticoats as much in evidence on the streets as the trimming of their head-wear. But this is running beauty into the ground, or very near to it, and for the present we dismiss the subject.

II.

AMERICANS IN PARIS.

THE number of American students who are rounding off their artistic training in Paris is variously estimated to be from 1,500 to 2,000. Many come here to perfect themselves in the French language, and as most of these have a teaching career in view, they are wise in getting their knowledge of French from the French people. For practical purposes, this is the only way in which the language can be acquired. Lessons are very cheap. You can get good teaching in private for a few dollars a week, and in classes for a few francs; and, of course, the great advantage of being in Paris is that, while you are finishing off in the theory, you can confirm yourself in what you learn by daily practice in the school of experience.

Another contingent of the American art colony is that which has a musical career before it. With these it is a proverb that, up to a certain point, New York affords as good instruction for the singer as any Continental city, but that beyond that point the best results can be obtained only in Paris. To speak as the students themselves do, the final difference between Paris and New York is the difference between a voice worth a hundred dollars a night and the same voice rounded out into dimensions and capabilities which make it worth twice that sum. Perhaps, though, this doubling of it marketable value is due less to any new quality of the voice itself than to the prestige one acquires from having studied abroad. Lessons in singing are much more costly than those in language. The great teachers of vocalism charge five dollars to be troubled with you for only half an hour. This, however, is little, if any, in excess of the highest New York figures; and were it not for the outside expenses, the outlay might not be a bad investment. But singers have to live better than other students. The first requisite is prime physical health, and this means good apartments and a good table—things which, in Paris, cost a lot of money. An acquaintance, who is having a practical experience of all this, estimates that his half-hour lessons at five dollars, three a week, are costing him altogether, including his tickets from home and back, about twenty-five dollars apiece.

There are a number of young Americans studying architecture over here, and a few carving out an education in sculpture; but the majority are novitiates of the brush and easel. The latter find in Paris facilities which are unsurpassed, and are afforded the best possible teaching for the lowest imaginable outlay. There are two things which these budding American geniuses never tire of extolling. One is the substantial patronage given to art by the French Government, and the other is the fact that the French masters are so generous toward students from other nations. There is nothing national about French painting except the glory and the pecuniary profits of it. Her schools and studios are open to the world, and, with only a few exceptions, the prizes of her grand *salon* are as accessible to foreign genius as that of her own sons. Americans seem to be accorded a special welcome to the artistic opportunities offered here, and one can not be long in a company of American artists or art students without learning that this gracious predilection is gratefully and even enthusiastically reciprocated.

There are three courses open to the art student in Paris. He may connect himself with a private school, of which the city boasts many which are excellent; or, he may obtain admission, if he can, to the *Ecole des Beaux Arts*; or, again, he may do both, if he choose, at the same time. The American student generally inclines to the first of these, and you will oftener than not find him attached to one of the popular Julian schools, of which there are several in different parts of the city for both sexes. Under this system a work-room is afforded him, in which he can ply his profession for a certain number of hours every day, and where, twice a week, he will have the benefit of the best artistic criticism—all for an outlay of about five dollars a month. The mode of entry into the *Beaux Arts* is, to exhibit one's drawings to some professor. If the view is satisfactory, you are installed as an "aspirant," or person on trial. Then, your progress being what it should, you are promoted gradually from the *Antique* to the *Atelier*, and become eligible, in due course, to compete for distinguished honors and large premiums. The cost for all this is nothing. Once a year the classes give a dinner to their professors. The student will, of course, subscribe to that; but as he will probably, in a six months' residence, have acquired some of the French propensity for gormandizing, he will look upon this outlay as being less a recompense to his teacher than a treat to himself.

A curious fact about art students is that, in private schools, aspirants of the female sex are charged nearly double the fee exacted from young men. Still more curious is the reason assigned for this. French professors, it is said, do not like to criticise the work of women, and because the task is a disagreeable one, they demand better pay for performing it. Here is an instance in which the proverbial gallantry of the French character pays. Certainly it pays the professors; though, when one remembers how much these gentlemen do solely from the love of art, and how low comparatively are their very highest demands for tribute, it is impossible to be severe upon them. None the less, it seems a pity that the Frenchman's reverence for woman should work in this way to her disadvantage.

Speaking of the ladies, one can not help admiring

the good work being done for American students of that sex by the Rev. W. R. Newell and his wife. The beginning of this good work was in little informal gatherings, on Sabbath evenings, within the domicile of this worthy couple, and its existing dimensions are seen in the suite of rooms—something in the nature of clubrooms—maintained for our fair compatriots, at 19 Rue Vevin. The moneyed power behind this enterprise is Mrs. Whitelaw Reid; but the originators and the real sustainers of it are Mr. and Mrs. Newell. The rooms are open all day; and many are the American girls who, worn out with hard work and made homesick by their disappointments, seek occasional asylum and refreshment within them. Good reading is afforded, with no end of kind sympathy and good advice. Every evening tea is served to those who choose to partake of it, and every Sabbath evening there is a service of song, followed by a warm-hearted, fatherly sort of talk from the good clergyman; and after that come lemonade and cake, which are passed around amid the hum and stir of a regular American sociable. It goes without the saying that to these formal gatherings on Sunday, and to such delightful entertainments as are always gotten up at Thanksgiving and Christmas, the young men are invited. It may be added also that to Young America, turned loose in the gay city of Paris, such opportunities for pure intercourse, under wholesome restraints, with girls of their own nationality and sometimes of their own neighborhood, mean more than words can express.

In regard to young men, it is questionable if some do not come to Paris who might better be kept much nearer to maternal apron-strings. Indulgent friends have given them an excessive idea of their own talent, and they come here—a few do—to find before long that, at best, they can not rise above the mediocre. This is discouraging, and occasionally even ruinous. Besides, Paris is a dreadful place for a young man of small will-power and pliable habits. It can surely do no harm to warn those interested of the moral risks lying in the pathway of the Paris art student. We more than suspect that, at present, ambitious parents do not always give sufficient consideration to these things. Still, it is only the few who make shipwreck on this turbulent sea. The boys, as a rule, are well-behaved. Most of them have neither the time nor the money for great excesses; and many are so well poised, both morally and intellectually, that the incitements to a fast life are no more felt in this city of pleasure than in the quiet life they might be living at home.

Many of these gifted American boys we have seen, and candor compels the admission that they are a noble class, if one may judge from appearances. Broad, high foreheads, clean-cut lips, and eyes which beam with intelligence,—these are their usual characteristics. They have quite a distinguished look, as a rule, and some bear unmistakable marks of genius. In a room full of such young men, one can not help speculating upon their future. American art is only emerging from its infancy. Here are the men whose gifts and accomplishments will help it before long into an honorable manhood. All will not achieve greatness; but some will, and their names and works will command national and even international applause. Some of them, however, are having hard times just now. We have heard of those who are eking out a subsistence upon as little as twenty cents a day, including a bed to sleep in—such as it is. These, of course, are exceptions, but there are many who get along upon a yearly expenditure of three or four hundred dollars. This, in Paris, means a room under the roof, probably in the fifth or sixth story, and the most frugal table, not to speak of other necessary economies. Rather a hard life, but borne cheerfully by those who can do no better; and some of the girls fare just as poorly as the most impecunious of the boys.

Upon eight or nine hundred a year, the student will get along very well. The Chanler scholarships, recently instituted, are on the $900 basis, and they are hailed by the students as the beginning of better times for at least a few of them. Among the girl students it is not uncommon for several to live together and keep house. This is pleasant, but somewhat dangerous; for the girls, it is said, are liable, under such an arrangement as this, not to eat at regular times, nor in sufficient quantity, the result being that health gives way. At a recent reception, given at the girls' club-rooms, an address was made by the American minister, Mr. Coolidge. To an outsider it seemed strange to hear him advising these high-spirited American damsels upon so commonplace a matter as their eating; but when he insisted upon their not putting themselves off with "less than three meals a day, *every day*," and all the girls tittered at the remark, every one turning to look knowingly at her neighbor, one could well understand the need for such advice.

As to the way in which the boys live, it may be said generally, allowing for exceptions, that they room in an attic and take their meals at twenty-five-cent restaurants. We make this statement upon the testimony of the students themselves. But in regard to eating, they are better off than they used to be, because of the good, cheap fare provided at a restaurant which is practically under their own control. This is attached to the American Art Students' Club, an institution founded about a year ago by Mr. A. A. Anderson, a distinguished American artist resident in Paris. The location of this Club is right in the center of the students' quarter, at 131 Boulevard Montparnasse, and it affords to the young men similar facilities, barring the religious element, to those which the young women enjoy in a locality a few squares away. Here, as at the other place, there are occasional entertainments—a male party one fortnight, and the next, a party in which the ladies share. Thus, while student life in Paris has its dangers and hardships, it has also its brighter aspects; and it will be gratifying to Americans to be assured that the city which has so long held out to their gifted sons and daughters so many artistic inducements, is offering now, in connection with these, a few social and moral safeguards.

III.

ON THE BOULEVARDS.

PARISIAN life, as seen on the Great Boulevards, has often been described, but the subject has lost none of its fascination for either the visitor or the reader; and as no two visitors look at the scene from precisely the same standpoint, or are impressed by just the same things, there is still a chance for one who shall sketch this scene from personal observation to make his pictures both original and interesting. By the Great Boulevards we mean the streets bearing that name which were constructed under Louis XIV, and which extend in almost a complete circle around what was formerly the city, their site having originally been the location of the city ramparts, or fortifications. Outside of these there is another circle of boulevards, and this circle marks the site of the ramparts of Paris after they had been extended so as to embrace the former suburbs, or Faubourgs. Still farther out, beyond the Communes, and at the extreme limits of what is the Paris of to-day, are those boulevards, so-called, which form a sort of military road for the massing of troops, and the manning and victualing of the mammoth defenses by which the Paris of the future hopes to protect itself more effectually than it did twenty-two years ago against any possible incursion of the armies of Kaiser William. Thus the city has an abundance of boulevards; and one is tempted to remark, apropos of the derivation of this name from *bulwarks*, that if all these great thoroughfares furnished as many evidences of the things which conduce to national strength as they do of the prevailing passion for adornment, this wonderful city would be well fortified indeed, both against external foes and against the more subtle and dangerous forces which menace her from within.

Chief among the Great Boulevards are those which bear the names of Madeleine, Capucines, Italiens, Montmartre, Poissonnièr, Bonne-Nouvelle, and St. Denis. An afternoon's saunter along these thoroughfares, keeping the eyes open and the reflective faculties busy *en route*, will reveal to you very much that is characteristic of this gay city. You will get in such a walk a good view of Parisian life, will pass or be within sight of many places of commanding interest, and will be reminded repeatedly of the checkered and sanguinary history the city has had. Almost everything in Paris speaks of change and violence, and this idea is made strikingly prominent in our walk on the Great Boulevards. We start at the Church of St. Mary Magdalen—the *Madeleine*. It was intended originally to be, what it now is, a place of worship; but Bonaparte converted it into a Temple of Glory. Begun in 1777, it was retarded in its erection by two Revolutions (1792 and 1830), and was not finally finished until 1842. Here is a reminder both of the vicissitudes of the nation and of the vacillating attitude of the national Government toward religion.

This is at the beginning of our walk; and at the other end, within a few hundred yards of each other, are two grim-looking piles which are similarly suggestive, and in their modern history even more so. These are the *Portes* St. Denis and St. Martin, erected by the city in honor of the victories of the Grand Monarch. In 1814, after the first overthrow of Napoleon, the Allied Armies entered the city by the Porte St. Martin. A fearful desecration, and it marked a great change; but it was a scene of peace, and quite an affair of honor, in comparison with the scenes these two *Portes* witnessed during the ravages of the last Commune. The *Place de l'Opera* marks the site of another great change, and one, happily, which it is a pleasure to recall. When you stand in this *Place*, which has no less than six broad thoroughfares diverging from it, and remember that from the ground now left vacant for convenience and pleasure some five hundred houses had to be removed at almost untold cost, you get a practical object-lesson of what Parisian enterprise means; and when you look at the grand opera-house itself, which covers three acres and cost nearly ten millions of dollars, your conception of what has been done to make Paris the most beautiful city in the world is enlarged still further.

Even here, though, spite of the beauty and enterprise about you, it is impossible to lose sight of that which has been horrible in this city's history, or to divest yourself entirely of fear for her future. At the other end of the grand Rue de la Paix the Column Vendôme rises to your view, looking as though it had stood there undisturbed for a hundred years. Yet in 1871 the fury of a Parisian mob had leveled it to the ground; and not far beyond is the site of the Tuileries, to which Parisian madmen applied, at the same time, the torch of the incendiary. Even the paving of these great streets has its story of foreboding to tell. It is no longer of stone, because so often stones have been used for barricades and weapons of assault, but of wood, and in the smallest blocks, the peculiar rumbling of the traffic over it, which reminds you at first of the rumbling sound peculiar to the ocean, seeming, in consequence, like a never-ceasing admonition at once of what has been and what may be.

But the shops you see on these boulevards give no sign of anything like this; and the throngs of people you meet are surely, for the greater part, living neither in the past nor the future, but in the gay and all-engrossing present. You detect no fear in the air; but you do often detect in it the real or artificial fragrance of flowers. This is distinctly Parisian. We never noticed it to any extent in New York, nor in London, but we pass shop after shop in Paris which sends out a delightful fragrance to us; and occasionally a creature in silks and ribbons will sweep past, so bountifully endued with perfume as to infect the air with sweetness for yards behind her. If it were only possible, as these Parisian ladies pass by, leaving such delightful reminders in their wake, to dismiss from your mind the old saying that where odors of this kind are used so freely you may suspect the presence of others which it is desirable to conceal, one could not only be thankful to these fragrant creatures, but might almost be in danger of admiring them.

What the feminine complexion is like in Paris, one can hardly say from a walk on the boulevards. The furtive glances we have ventured to cast upon it have left the impression that you see it in public under a mask; but the mask is exceedingly pretty as a work of art. Those who have seen this complexion at early breakfast say that the mask, so generally and so skillfully put on later in the day, is more attractive than the face itself would be. Perhaps it is; but to give these Parisian ladies their due, it must be added that their faces are well formed, that most of them are blessed with the loveliest eyes, and that they maintain altogether a very pleasing and even striking expression. In the latter characteristic the proud dames of old England look dull and insipid, as a rule, in comparison with their fair sisters of sunny France; and we are not sure that the Parisian beauty is fully equaled, in this one point of wearing habitually a gentle and pleasing expression, by even the best types among our own countrywomen.

But we are digressing to talk of the ladies—not at all an uncommon weakness in Paris, especially with men who spend much time on the Great Boulevards. But in our present description of these great arteries of life there are other beautiful things to be noted. In fact, everything is beautiful, and everything is obviously designed to be so. The shops which most attract you are those in which articles of luxury for the household are displayed. If French *salons* are furnished after the models you see on the boulevards, what nests of elegance and art they must be! After looking into windows where bonnets and dress-goods are displayed, you hardly wonder at the passion of Paris for pretty toilets, or at the craze which has made this city the shopping emporium of the world. In the tempting display of *bric-a-brac* the Parisian shopkeeper is simply overwhelming. Even the butchers' shops are beautiful. Fancy the interior of a dressed calf decked out with roses! Think of sheep, waiting to be cut up, with dainty paper caps over their necks, with pretty pictures adorning their backs, and with a green leaf, having an ornamental gilt center, at the base of their tails! This is Paris, whether you see it on the boulevards or on the back streets; and what you observe in one line of trade, fairly represents the artistic genius of shopkeepers in general.

If by any chance, in sauntering along the boulevards, you should grow weary of looking at other beautiful things, you can turn at any moment and look at yourself, for mirrors seem to be everywhere. Not only has the shopkeeper provided them abundantly in his show-windows; but they are on the doors, on the sides of the entry way, and in every other available place. Evidently, too, this ample provision meets a widespread want. We had thought it only a weakness of the fair sex to have a fondness for looking-glasses, but Paris has disabused us of this notion. On the boulevards it is almost as common to see men worshiping at this shrine as to see women standing in adoration before it. We are not prepared as yet to say that the well-dressed Frenchman is vain; but the care he bestows upon his facial adornment, and particularly upon his mustache, has raised within us a suspicion of this kind, and the *penchant* he shows for posing before these public and ever-present mirrors has somewhat strengthened that suspicion.

To start again at the Madeleine, you notice at once how the broad sidewalks are dotted at short intervals by pretty booths. These are newspaper-stands, and places where flowers can be bought. Occasionally you pass a high, circular contrivance, around the top of which is the word "Spectacles." These are for the display of theatrical bills, and at night they are illuminated from the top. This is how Paris modifies and makes pleasing those bill-sticking propensities which in American cities are allowed full play, regardless of both taste and decency. But other objects on the sidewalk, found at intervals of about a couple of squares, and standing out as conspicuously on the crowded boulevards as elsewhere, will prompt you to compare American cities with Paris to the decided advantage of the former, and will make you thankful that in certain matters we still retain, on our side of the ocean, a measurable sense of delicacy.

Which reminds us, however, that our own country is represented on these boulevards, and not always at its best. There are places where they advertise American drinks; and in the vicinity of the Grand Hotel you may easily pick up one of your compatriots as a guide in doing the sights of this gay city. These are questionable advantages—the latter as much so as the former. But no American can notice without pride the gaping crowd of Parisians which constantly surrounds a shop in the Boulevard des Italiens, where American type-writers are on exhibition.

Making your way toward the other end of this string of boulevards you observe, after a time, that the scene has changed somewhat, that the shops are less sumptuous, and the living figures in this stirring panorama of life less fashionably attired. Here you see many who belong to the great army of Parisian toilers; and in regard to the women, you will be struck by the large numbers of this class, daintily dressed otherwise, who will be bareheaded. This is another Paris fashion; but there is hardly enough in it for milliners to secure it a place in the fashion-plates of America. Perhaps as you return toward the Madeleine, the scene will have changed still more by the fact of darkness having called into play the myriad lights which make these boulevards even more fascinating than in daytime. But Paris by night we do not care to dwell upon.

IV.

THE POOR OF PARIS.

THE public ball-rooms of Paris have furnished many a salacious morsel for American readers. They are still in full blast; and, judging from the pictures one can see in a hundred windows of this city, they are still presenting nightly to Parisian youth the same old scenes of female indecency. We were recently, however, in one of these rooms which is used now for a totally different purpose. The gallery is there from which, in former years, the eyes of lust looked down upon dancers whose attitudes and movements ministered to the lowest passions; but these galleries are occupied at present by those seeking a better life, and are adorned in front with mottoes from the Holy Word. On the ground-floor we find now, instead of the gay votaries of vice, a decent assemblage of middle-aged dames, with a bright intermingling of innocent, clean-faced childhood. It is a Mothers' Meeting, held under the auspices of the great McAll. The women are all poor, but they look very clean and remarkably intelligent. Most of the two hundred have brought their knitting with them, and the diligent plying of their needles, while a young lady reads to them some wholesome story, is a reminder to us of how, in the gathering storm of a hundred years ago, the women of Paris used to knit into their work the names of those whom their revolutionary vengeance had marked for the guillotine. But what a change since then, we reflect, and how delightfully suggestive is the scene we now behold of the revolution which is quietly going on in these days in the morals and habits of these Parisian women!

In our visit to this interesting place we were accompanied by a gentleman whose knowledge of the poor of this great city has been gained by many years of self-sacrificing labor for their advancement; and when we saw over the door of this erstwhile ball-room, "*Salle New York*," indicating that the work done in this particular locality was backed by American means, we felt quite sure that what our guide could tell us and show us of lowly life in Paris, and of what is being done to redeem it, would be as welcome to the better class of American readers as other and less innocent views are to readers who delight in having scandal and vice described to them.

"The poor of Paris," began our friend—"well, they are not so vulgar, not so brutal, not so drunken, as the poor of London. They are more self-respecting, and will make altogether a better impression upon you." This was the opinion of one who is proud of old England as his native country, and it is a view which is fully borne out by our own observations. "How do they live? Well, to begin with, they have scarcely any home comforts. That's why they are on the streets so much. Of fire, they have next to none, and lights the same. The candle or two they may keep about are brought into service only when some one drops in. Cooking? Why, the very poor hardly ever do any. They get their food from the numerous little shops where meat and vegetables are sold ready for the table. Cheap? No, meat is not, unfortunately; but vegetables are, and these form the staple of their living. Perhaps, by the way, you've visited the great markets, and have noticed the stalls there where plates of cooked edibles are sold at four sous (four cents) apiece. These are eagerly snatched up as special delicacies. They are scraps from the tables of the wealthy. How collected? Well, it is something of a mystery; but there they are, and it is generally supposed that they are obtained for a trifling bounty through the servants."

So our friend talked on, and occasionally, as we jogged together through the narrow and crooked thoroughfares in the neighborhood of Rue St. Antoine, he would call our attention to something particularly squalid or ancient in our surroundings. We should not find here, he said, many of the very poor. It was not the worst part of the city; but it approximated to that distinction, and it had some features not to be found anywhere else. The district is known as "Old Paris." Before the time of the Grand Monarch the French nobility dwelt in this quarter. What were palaces then are now either *magazines* of trade or common tenement-houses. Several mediæval towers were pointed out to us, one of which is associated with the murder, by the Duke of Burgundy, of the brother of a French king. We saw, also, the old palace which for long years was the residence of the archbishops of the Seine. Now the courts of this vast structure resound to the tread of poverty, and its massive stairways are climbed by those who seek, in hunger, rooms which are bare and cold. For the narrowness of some of its thoroughfares this part of the city—which, by the way, is seldom seen by visitors—is without an equal. A small alley was pointed out to us as the narrowest street in all Paris. It is not more than a yard and a half in width, and only that its name, with the ubiquitous "Rue," is plainly given on the walls of its high buildings, you would not suspect it of being a street at all. But we saw several not more than three yards wide. On either side, too, were the inevitable five and six story dwelling-houses. Which moves us to remark that the poor of Paris are worse off than the poor of London in some respects. They certainly have less light, and a deal more climbing to do. This, because the dwellings are so much higher. We are still of the opinion, and in fact are more fully confirmed in it, that, for the necessity of stair-climbing it imposes, Paris beats the world. In this matter, poor and rich are sufferers almost equally; and one wonders that, with such decided revolutionary tendencies, the people here have never yet taken up arms against tyrannical architects.

Our kind cicerone was too much occupied with good work for the poor of Paris to give a whole afternoon to the mere task of showing an inquisitive American where and how they live. Hence, he mingled business with pleasure, so to speak. In other words, he had made out a calling-list, and, fortunately for us, we were to share these domiciliary visits. But still he talked. "One thing about the working-people of Paris," he said, "is very noteworthy and highly commendable. They wear their own clothes—not the cast-off finery of the rich; and what they wear is neither ragged nor dirty." We had thought as much, and remarking upon the large number of women who go about the streets bareheaded, our friend observed: "That is a matter of economy. See the same people on a bright Sunday or other gala-day, or at a place of worship, and you will find them looking quite differently. A neat bonnet will appear; and, as for the men, they must be low down indeed not to have a respectable suit for holiday wear. But they understand economy. They are different, in that respect, from the poorer classes in England. The bonnet, which costs something and looks well, must be taken care of and made to last. So with the best suit of the man. Hence these are not worn except on great occasions, and never when it rains."

"The last uprising of the Commune," we suggested—

"was it shared in actively by the people among whose abodes we are now moving?" To which our friend replied that it was not. "The working-people here are scattered about amongst classes that are better off. Consequently they have less opportunity to become clannish. Their social views are modified somewhat by their surroundings. The really dangerous classes are in places like Belleville, where vast hordes of workmen are huddled together, and where the spirit of these toiling thousands, aggregated and solidified, is a dominating power in social and municipal life."

All of which was exceedingly instructive; but just here we followed our friend into the hallway of a tenement, and the ever-watchful *concierge*, or porter, having been satisfied as to the propriety of our intentions, we groped our way up five flights of stairs. The building had formerly been a mansion, and so thick was the railing that to clasp it with the hand, as a help to our ascent, was impossible. But it was so dark, and the ascent was so steep, that we could hardly have gotten along without some help of this kind. Hence it was a relief to find that landlords, in this quarter, had been required by law to attach to these ancient railings a thinner rail of iron. By such assistance as we got from one of these, we found ourselves at last in the apartment of a Paris workman—one who, unfortunately, had been out of employment for some time, with a sick wife on his hands.

Here was the abode of honest poverty. It was a single room, but was made double by curtains. The curtains were an exact match in color and pattern for the blue-tinted wall-paper. This was only to be expected; for to combinations and matches—the little things which indicate a prevailing taste for the beautiful and artistic—the poor of Paris are as passionately devoted, within their means, as are the rich and leisured. The apartment was rented as a furnished one for eight francs a week; but the furniture was anything but abundant, and the bedstead was of a plain iron pattern. In its size the family was typically Parisian. It consisted of a bright-looking girl of ten years. The working-people of France, we have before remarked, are economical, and here is a practical illustration of the sort of economy on their part which is giving so much trouble these days to the social economists of this country. Kind words from the good missionary, with a short invocation, introduced by the familiar "*Notre pere;*" a hearty *Bon jour*, which means "Good day;" and a hand-shake, which meant to the *bonne dame* that she would be better off thereafter to the extent of a modest silver coin,—so began and so ended our first visit. It was brief, but it gave us a touching view of French home-life, and a delightful insight into the good work of Protestant missionaries in this city.

Another call had an element of genuine romance in it. We were forewarned of the situation, but the curious dénouement was quite unexpected. "Don't trouble yourself if the good woman cries a bit," our friend had said. "She's poor, and she's in trouble. A man wants to marry her; but he's out of work, and I'm discouraging the match. My visit to-day is for that special object." Here were grand possibilities opening before us; and we entered the apartment prepared for anything, as we thought, and yet hardly prepared for what really took place. The woman was fat, not fair, and much beyond forty; but she was tidily dressed, and in her trim black cap looked matronly enough to be not only a wife, but the mother of a lot of olive-branches.

In what took place during this visit we were imposed upon, owing to our imperfect knowledge of French. But though the language deceived us, our eyes did not. We were quite sure that we saw a third man enter the apartment, and that, after an introduction to the visitor from America, he proceeded to make himself very much at home. We were sure, also, that there was a general and very animated conversation, and that the new-comer, in sustaining his own special part therein, became nervous, and had recourse frequently to his snuff-box. We also heard a little prayer, and, as we had been forewarned, saw a woman in tears. Then we saw the good dominie sign a paper, and afterwards he read from a familiar-looking book what sounded very much like a familiar benediction. Then parting salutations were exchanged; and afterwards, when the court-yard had been gained, the astonishing explanation came.

Actually, this kind clergyman, while swearing he'd ne'er consent, had consented on the spot. He couldn't help it, he said, because they pleaded so eloquently. "We're both poor," the man had urged, "and we're both miserable as we are. She comes home, and finds no comfort; I go home, and there is no comfort for me. Let us share our miseries, and see if in that way we may not lighten them." So the man, happening to drop in, had urged his suit; with such success, too, that the paper which had been signed was the document which will be presented to the mayor, by and by, as the last preliminary in the civil features of a French marriage.

"So there are some marriages in France where the bride brings no dowry?" we remarked. To which our cicerone replied that, of course, there were such weddings among the poor, though even with the poorest there would be a strict inventory of the little belongings of the two parties; and the bride would have a *dot* really, or what would be considered such, though she brought to the union only the clothes she stood up in.

"But marriage—marriage," said our friend, "is made so difficult in France that it is no wonder there is widespread concubinage. The formalities of the law are outrageous. Many are the Frenchmen who have said to me that had they known beforehand what annoyances they would have to submit to, they would not have undertaken it. My own daughter was married to a Frenchman, and here is what I had to do: To satisfy the authorities that the girl was not some French damsel wishing to evade the customary requirements in such cases, I had to get her certificate of baptism. This had to be translated by a sworn translator, and the prefect of police had to swear that this sworn translator was all right. Then, the British consul had to swear that the certificate of baptism was all right; and, finally, the French minister of foreign affairs had to take oath that the British consul was all right. For all of which, as a matter of course, I had to pay.

"And here," he continued, "is this case we have just left. Both are beyond fifty; yet both must have the consent of their parents, or must show good reason why it can not be obtained. The man's parents are dead; but he had to prove it, which was very difficult. The woman has a mother living; but she is eighty-seven, and in her dotage. Nevertheless she must consent; and all these preliminaries had been arranged at last, but only after a three months' campaign." Our friend was indignant; and we rather suspect that his antipathy to the French marriage-laws, and his own painful experience with them, had a little to do in evoking his consent to the union of the couple we had just visited.

About dusk we saw the school children returning home, looking quite as tidy as the little toddlers in our own cities, and all, like our own, carrying their little bags of school-books with them. Still later we entered a common lodging-house, and our guide introduced us to a converted absinthe-drinker. Some years ago he drank thirty-six glasses of that nerve-destroying decoction at a single sitting. It was done for a wager. Results—three months in hospital, and a wrecked constitution. Instead of inflating himself with drink, he now inflates with wind the organ of an adjacent mission-hall, and peddles oranges for a living. The neighborhood about here was very hard, and the thought occurred to us that our friend had hitched on to his hard-looking convert just then to keep us in countenance while we passed through it. But soon we found ourselves in the grand *place* of the Hotel de Ville; and here, after a cup of coffee together, we took passage for our respective homes.

V.

PARIS AND ITS SUBURBS.

ROUND about Paris there is a circle of fortifications, surrounded on the outside by a deep excavation which, in case of a siege, could be filled in a short time by a mighty barrier of water. The approaches to the city are commanded by more than fifty forts, and the garrison of defense numbers fifty thousand picked men. These, and kindred facts, have just won for Paris a decided compliment. The chancellor of the German Empire has said recently that it is the best protected city in the world. From such a source this is high praise indeed. The French are like ourselves in one thing. Not only have they a high opinion of their own achievements, but they like to feel that what they do is generously estimated by others. Especially proud are they of their big city on the Seine; and, as everybody knows, they have the most substantial reasons for wishing Germany to think well of that city—particularly of its defenses. Count Von Caprivi has not promised that the armies of the Kaiser will never again subdue Paris, but he has praised the city, and has really conferred upon it a new distinction. For beauty and gayety it has long held the palm; and now, if one may accept in such a matter the judgment of a nation which a couple of decades ago forced an entrance through her gates, Paris the beautiful may add to her former laurels the proud title of excelling all other cities from a military point of view.

At present, however, the gates and fortifications of Paris seem to be useful principally for the levying of vexatious taxes upon the French people themselves. Of this we were forcibly reminded, one day, as we approached the Porte Mallot, in company with a gentleman who was on his way to fill a lecture engagement at the Sorbonne. Our friend carried a bag containing a few books he was intending to use, and the question to be settled before we could pass was whether anything in the bag was taxable. To satisfy the gatekeeper, the bag must be opened. It was all done quickly enough, and with evident politeness; but it struck the American mind quite unfavorably, and, of course, provoked it to numerous inquiries. Paris, it appears, lays tribute in this way upon almost her entire food-supply, and upon numerous other things; and the money collected is divided between the Government and the municipal authorities. By this means it comes to pass that many articles are doubly taxed; for in addition to what is assessed upon them at the gates of the city, there is the tariff imposed at the frontier.

After this we did not wonder that a visitor had to pay so enormously for apartments and board, though we did wonder at the long-suffering patience of the residents. Meat of every kind is taxed. On a pound of butter the city tariff is three cents, and on a pound of grapes it is about the same. If you should go outside and shoot a hare, you would have to pay for bringing into Paris even a private little acquisition of that sort. Upon spirits and wine the duty is considerable, and the authorities are exceedingly vigilant in collecting it. This is a point at which vigilance is quite necessary, judging from what one hears as to the methods of smuggling in vogue. We are told that during the cholera scare, liquors were surreptitiously brought in by means of coffins; and we have heard of one enterprising liquor-dealer who cheated the Government for a long time by means of a dummy footman. That is, he had a wooden contrivance on the seat of his carriage, shaped and dressed like a footman; and this innocent-looking luxury was filled, not with animal spirits, but with the kind which, at the gates of Paris, are held to be contraband.

These ruses were decidedly clever, and it is said that had it not been for accomplices who turned informers they might have continued in successful operation indefinitely. Perhaps, however, the countryman's ruse was the most effectual for the time, though it must have put him to inconvenience afterwards. He had only a bottle of common wine with him; but the gatekeeper knew his duty, and did it. The tax was four cents, levied upon an original valuation of something like twelve cents. Common wine, it must be remembered, is very cheap in France; and this particular bottle would have been cheap enough, one might have thought, even after the duty had been paid. But the French peasant is noted for his thrift. The burning question was how to get his quart of wine into Paris without any further investment upon it, and the final solution was reached by his carrying it through the gates concealed, as in the case of the dummy footman, within his own anatomy.

From the fact of the fifty-five gates which admit to Paris being used as so many tax-gathering offices, it naturally follows that the necessaries of life are much cheaper on the outside; and this, in turn, accounts for the large number of thriving communities which nestle so thickly about the walls of this city. Le Vallois-Perret, the largest of these, has forty thousand inhabitants; Boulogne has thirty thousand; Neuilly, twenty-five thousand; and Vincennes, twenty thousand. The dozen or more others are not so large, but they are all up into the thousands; and some of them, in their pretty villas and other rural features, present a contrast to Paris which is very delightful. For the greater part, however, these outskirts of the city bear a too-monotonous resemblance in their architecture to the city itself.

The advantage of living in these villages is, that you are at the doors of Paris, with all that it offers of life and opportunity, and still are exempt, in a measure, from the burden of Parisian prices. Unfortunately, however, you miss here the public spirit and what may be called the official cleanliness of Paris. Parisian streets are cleaned every day; those in the suburbs enjoy this treat at odd times, and some of them apparently after long intervals. And another drawback to suburban residence is, that if you use either cabs, omnibuses, or other public conveyances, you will find that, alike in entering and leaving, the city gates will invariably impose an extra fare upon you. Which reminds us again that the gates of Paris are eminently a business institution. They are not for ornament alone, nor are they kept up merely as a safeguard against possible incursions from Germany; but they are decidedly a means of revenue, and in the tribute they lay upon people and things outside, they seem to corroborate the old notion that Paris is superior to France.

Paris is entered by ten railways, and its extremities are connected with each other by what is known as the railway of the circle. *Chemin de fer de Ceinture* is the French name, and this road makes a circuit of the city just within the fortifications. The distance covered is twenty-three miles. There are thirty stations. Most of the track is below the level of the streets. There are only, however, five tunnels, and the longest is not more than three-quarters of a mile. Elsewhere the road is higher than the streets. This Parisian *chemin de fer* is far more pleasant to travel on than the gloomy underground railways of London; and, spite of the fact that there is no third class, traveling upon it is reasonably cheap. The lowest fare is six cents, but you can go two or three miles for that sum; and for eleven cents you can cover the full length of the line. Outside the city there is another circular railway. This is the *Chemin de fer de Grande Ceinture.* The nearest it comes to the fortifications is at Bobigny, where it is within two miles, and it is at its greatest distance at St. Germain, where it is seven miles away.

For getting about in the city itself, the arrangements are varied enough, but they are very slow as a rule, and some of them are distressingly old-fashioned. This is hardly the age of electricity in Paris. There are few streets lighted by this means, and you have to search with great diligence to find an electric-car. The only vehicles offering you any approach to rapid transit are the steam-trams. But these also are few; and thus, if you are too economical to "cab it," you are entirely at the mercy of vehicles which travel only a little faster than a healthy man could easily walk. But the ticket system which obtains here is highly commendable. You get your number in the order in which you arrive at the station where the bus or tram is to stop. Perhaps you are a weak little woman. Before the vehicle comes along, a dozen or two men may have taken tickets; but if you were the first, you have the first right to a seat; and this is all attended to so carefully and quietly that there is no chance for cheating, and no occasion for crowding.

If the notice "Complete" is put up before your number is reached, you will, of course, be a little disappointed; but how it will delight you, upon reflection, to find trams and busses which sometimes do get to be absolutely full! In American cities there is always room for one more, even when the last man to jump on is still hanging by the bell-rope; but here it is so many—the number which can be comfortably accommodated—and not one more. Apropos of the sign "Complete," and of what it means, there is a good story of an Irishman—probably an American Irishman—who, in recounting his Parisian peregrinations, said he had been to every place about the city but Complate, and, bejabers, though he'd tried a hundred times to get a bus that was going there, he had never succeeded. He had often jumped upon the platform of such busses, but had always been ordered off.

In Paris you will waste your time if you look for a blonde-haired damsel every time you see a gray horse, for French girls are mostly of the brunette type; whereas gray horses are in the greatest profusion here, especially in public conveyances. There are forty lines of trams in this city, and nearly as many bus-lines; and, from long and close observation, we are driven to the conclusion that, taking the service through and through, the animals of a grayish complexion which are engaged in it are about three-fourths of the whole number. Paris is great on style, and this is its style in horse-hair.

Speaking of style in Parisian bus-horses reminds us, however, that the horses engaged in the enormous cab-service of this city are utterly without style. There are exceptions, of course; but, taken as a class, these animals are a sorry set—the least pleasing to the eye of anything you see in all this busy city. They are so numerous, too, that they form a leading feature on every thoroughfare; for Paris has ten thousand more cabs than London can boast, though London is twice the size of Paris. But the rate at which you can hire these Paris cabs—forty cents an hour, and less than that for a single journey—is eminently satisfactory; as also, barring the one feature of a runty-looking horse, is the general appearance of the vehicle itself.

And here we note, as another striking instance of the Parisian love of style, that generally there will be a match between the cab and the driver. If the cab is finished wholly in a dark shade, cabby's hat will be black. If the body of the cab is finished half-way up in a lighter shade—say in old gold, as many of them are—then cabby's hat will be white, with an old-gold band on it; and often you will notice, as the last straw which the most exacting fancy could desire, that this captivating French Jehu will be so mindful of artistic effects as to have a border of the same shade on the carriage-robe he wraps about him. This is decidedly Parisian, and is a fair sample of Paris life in all its varied aspects.

VI.

THE STREETS OF PARIS.

IN our study of the material aspects of Paris it has been a perennial source of pleasure, and a very great help, to find at every corner, within easy focus of the sidewalk, signs of uniform appearance, announcing in distinct characters the names of the various streets. In this matter the authorities have been so exact that, in making your way about, you feel like thanking them at every turn. And it is equally gratifying to find that the houses have been so carefully numbered, and that the numerals which mark them, instead of running continuously on one side of the street and then jumping to the other side and starting back, as they do in many other Continental cities, are arranged here on the convenient American plan of odds and evens opposite to each other.

Two things, however, have given us a little trouble. One is, that the numbers change so slowly, and that in searching for a particular domicile or shop one has to travel so far before reaching it. Speaking generally, Parisian houses are all large. This is because they are nearly all built for apartment houses. The typical Parisian lives in a flat. He will never speak to you of his home or his house, and in fact the use of such terms would be monstrously egotistical on his part; for the house he lives in is occupied, as a rule, by a dozen other families. Hence your home in Paris is always referred to—allowing for exceptions—as your *appartement*.

As for the typical Parisian house, this is really a block of houses extending around a court. It has a frontage of from seventy-five to one hundred and fifty feet, and stretches back a greater distance still. In height it is six stories, with another story in the roof. The windows are deep, and they all open like doors, window-sash being apparently quite unknown here. The only entrance from the street is a central archway. Penetrating this, you come at once to the lodge of the care-taker, or concierge. A little beyond, on both sides, are large stairways. If you pass into the courtyard you will find other stairways; and by means of these, if you have a very good pair of legs, you may hope to find your way gradually into the different compartments and rooms. Such a house as this you can see anywhere in Paris. It is the prevailing type. Rich and poor alike live in houses modeled upon this plan. And it is only the truth to say that if the reader will take our little sketch, and vary it somewhat—bearing in mind that nearly all the houses in this city have stone-fronts, real or imitation, that they all look as much alike as peas in the same pod, and that there are a sufficient number of them to pack closely some three or four thousand streets—he will have before him a tolerably correct view of what Paris is as a place of residence.

The other thing which troubles you a little in finding your way about Paris is the mania which the city fathers have developed for hauling down familiar street-names, and putting new ones up in their places. It is quite true that the names of the streets are in full view at every turning; but it does n't at all follow that the name you see to-day is the one your map gives, or the one which was there yesterday. It is affirmed, as an extreme instance, that the name of one street was changed three times within six months. The cause of this mania must be looked for in the extreme radical and secularistic sentiments of the municipal Council. These are republican times; hence names which stand for monarchy and oppression must give place to those those symbolizing progress and liberty.

It is also an era when the Catholic Church is not the supreme power it used to be—when, in fact, it has become the fate of that Church to receive from "the powers that be" annoyances rather than favors. Naturally, therefore, the names of numerous saints have had to go. Paris, however, is still sufficiently blessed, one would think, in the latter respect. How many saints' names have been hauled down, we are not apprised; but of the number remaining we have satisfied ourselves by a study of the Directory, our researches showing that the rues, boulevards, squares or *places*, in this city, which are still dignified by the name of some saint or saintess, amount in all to about an even hundred.

In regard to the naming of streets, that which especially delights the visitor from America is to find that several Parisian thoroughfares are named after the distinguished men of his own country. There is a Rue Washington, and, as every American would have wished, to keep that company there is a Rue Lincoln. These, of course, are in what is called, by courtesy, the American Quarter. Which reminds us, however, that the American colony in Paris is not so large as is generally supposed, our authority for this statement being a high official at the American Legation here. "How many Americans are resident in Paris during the winter season?" This was our question; the gentleman's reply being that estimates which put the number at twenty thousand, or even at ten thousand, were wild exaggerations. He was sure, indeed, that if the census were confined to those settled here for several months, it could not be placed truthfully at more than five thousand.

The American Quarter is in the Faubourg St. Honoré, that most beautiful part of Paris which embraces the Presidential Palace, the Champs Elysées, and the Arc de Triomphe. In this quarter, or very near to it, you find Churches holding service in English to the number of a dozen or more. Two of these are American Churches. Dr. Thurber, formerly of Syracuse,

New York, officiates at the pretty sanctuary in the Rue de Berri. This is a sort of Union Church. But the more stately building, in Ave de l'Alma, is of the Episcopal faith, the rector being Dr. Morgan, who has recently, by the way, established a mission for the benefit of American students in the Quartier Latin. It is gratifying to add that a deep interest is taken in American students by both these Churches, and that the two clergymen regard this as the most vital feature of their work. Dr. Thurber is pushing successfully a worthy plan for a new church-house. The property he wishes to acquire adjoins the church itself. It will be used primarily as a parsonage, but its secondary function will be as a sort of social and religious headquarters for that interesting section of the American colony which is rounding off its artistic education in this city.

Recurring to the streets of this wonderful city, the features one feels most inclined to dwell upon are such unique effects as you see in the Rue de Rivoli, where, for thirteen blocks, you pass under a canopied sidewalk, with tempting shop-windows on one hand, and on the other broad archways opening toward the Garden of the Tuileries. Then there are the numerous Passages, or Arcades, which are so distinctively a Parisian feature that they open to you in the most unlikely places, and seem often so sorry to have you leave them, that after ending their course on one side of the street, they immediately begin it again on the other side. Then, too, there is the marvelous Palais Royal, combining the best features of both the Rue de Rivoli and the Arcades. What other city is there which can show you such a place as that, with its striking architectural effects, its long array of jewelry-stores, its rich historical associations, and its thriving trade in articles of luxury and adornment?

Still other wonderful features of this captivating city are the length, breadth, and arrow-like straightness of some of its leading thoroughfares. One never wearies in his admiration of such Parisian effects as these; and here again it is Paris against the world. The Boulevard Voltaire extends, in a perfect line, from the Place de la République to the Place de la Nation, which is two miles; and for the eye to traverse this distance, either by gaslight or daylight, is an experience never to be forgotten. Another fine vista of a mile and a half is afforded by the Boulevard Magenta; and still another, almost as long, by the splendid boulevards of Sevastopol and Strasbourg; while, if it were not for a slight rise of ground at the center and the obstruction of your view by the Arc de Triomphe, you might stand at the Place de la Concorde, and follow with your eye, always looking in a straight line, first the Ave. des Champs Elysées, then the Ave. de la Grande Armée, after that and beyond the city gates the Ave. de Neuilly, and finally the Ave. de la Defense de Paris, until you saw the Bronze Monument, from which the last of these avenues takes its name,—the whole distance being four and a half miles!

One marvels that, after the late unpleasantness, there should remain in Paris a street bearing the name of Germany. So it is, however; though the soft French tongue calls this street the Rue d'Allemagne. Possibly this name is retained for the same reason that the ancients were wont to seat a skeleton at their banqueting-tables; namely, as a reminder to Parisian citizens of their impending conflict with a powerful enemy. It can hardly, however, symbolize to them all that a skeleton would imply; for, far from expecting to go under when they meet Germany for a second tussle, they are sanguine of a great triumph. But as to this street of Germany, we have referred to it because, with its connecting thoroughfare—Rue La Fayette—it affords another striking instance of the many beautiful streets in Paris which stretch out to great lengths in a straight line, the distance in this case being three miles and a quarter.

To get a passing view, in the shortest possible time and for the smallest outlay, of the principal places of interest in Paris, the best thing to do is to take a penny ride on the Seine. Think of it! Five and a half miles for only two cents, and a moving panorama as you skim along—the view being at close range withal— of the Jardin des Plantes, the Hotel de Ville, the Palais de Justice, the Louvre, the Institut, the Chambre des Deputies, the Hotel des Invalides, Tour Eiffel, and the Trocadèro! This is another respect in which Paris beats the world. The Seine is insignificant in comparison with the Thames, but you can see as you travel on it far more objects of interest than a penny ride on the London river will reveal to you; and, added to all, there is the delightful sensation of passing beneath twenty-five bridges during this cheap ride.

VII.

SOME PARISIAN NOVELTIES.

THAT the city which is the shopping-center of Europe, and which annually attracts to itself so many thousands of purchasers from America, should have in it the largest retail emporium to be found anywhere in the world, seems to accord perfectly with the natural fitness of things. This is the Bon Marché—Cheap Market; and it may safely be said that of all the objects of interest which Paris shows with pardonable pride to its throngs of admiring visitors, this is the one which exerts the greatest fascination over the feminine mind, and the one, moreover, which, from the fact just mentioned, has the most depleting effect upon the masculine pocket-book. We were told at Whiteley's big store in London that we could buy there anything from a toothpick to an elephant. It was also impressed upon us that, if we were in need of such a luxury, the proprietor would take an order to supply us with a wife; and that to furnish young men as dancers at evening parties, where the male sex would otherwise be inadequately represented, was a trade novelty in which that house did quite a thriving business. We have not discovered that the Bon Marché dabbles in such eccentricities as these, but it surely offers variety enough and what makes one's patronage of the place peculiarly satisfactory is that, in a city where tradesmen generally seem inclined to make you pay well for the misfortune of not being a native, and where, to a very large extent, the shops still do business on the bargain-and-barter system, this shop stands out as the most conspicuous of a very few where fixed prices prevail, where the notice, "English spoken," does not turn out to be a snare, and where Americans stand on an equal footing with Frenchmen at the cashier's desk.

Speaking, however, of the cashier's desk and of the privileges enjoyed there, reminds us of the curious fact that in Parisian shops the system of paying at the desk is so universal that even the Bon Marché does not vary from it. The clerk who waits upon you escorts you to this point of interest, and while one person receives your payment, another, not far away, wraps up your purchase; and during all this time you are still under the protecting care of the salesman, who finally leaves you only when you are in safe possession of both your change and your package, and are yourself taking leave of the store. To those who have been wont to look up in bewilderment while goods and money are flying automatically across the ceiling, this Parisian method appears to be old-fogyish and decidedly slow. You wonder, too, how such a dilly-dallying on the part of salesmen can ever pay. But in Europe clerk-hire is so low that it is cheaper in some cases than labor-saving machinery; and as to the time consumed, you do not find in practice that it is very great, while in stores like the Bon Marché, the aisles of which are always thronged, there is a decided advantage in removing the purchaser to another part when his order has been filled, because by that means additional room is left for customers who have yet to be served.

Like nearly all great enterprises, this big Parisian shop was built up from the most humble beginnings. Its projector was originally a peddler. Coming to Paris with a little capital—and with that which was still better, namely, a wife who, like most French women, had a genius for business—he established himself before long in a shop forty feet square, and, by the new fad of fixed prices and small profits, he gradually extended his operations until the peddler's pack he carried at his death was commensurate with one of the biggest blocks in Paris, representing a fabulous capital and an annual profit of millions of francs. For ten years after that, his widow carried on the business, the volume of trade still swelling and the profits still piling up, until, in 1888, she also died, the mammoth peddler's pack falling then upon those younger shoulders, which, with equal success and with increasing gain, are sustaining it at the present day.

But thereby hangs a tale, and one of the tenderest human interest—a tale which, in these days of big fortunes and little souls, ought to be proclaimed with trumpet voice in every market-place and along every avenue of commerce. The Bon Marché is not only a big business establishment, but a grand philanthropic enterprise. Aristide Boucicaut and his good wife, Marguerite, besides leaving the biggest shop in the world, have left to all the world an example of good works. Rarely has there been seen a greater aptitude for gathering enormous profits from legitimate trade; and for the lavish and practical way in which the earnings of this big business were turned back to benefit dependents and to bless a great city, the conduct of these Parisian shopkeepers has never been equaled. The principles which governed them were, that the first sharers in their vast success ought to be the faithful employees who helped to achieve it, and that after that they must remember substantially the community which had favored them with its confidence and patronage. Hence princely bounties at odd times for deserving clerks, and for a large number a partnership in the concern. Instead of fines for the infraction of trivial rules, a trust in the honor of the three or four thousand dependents, such as put every one upon his mettle, and inspired all with love and respect for the management. For the men after twenty years of service, and the women after fifteen years, a comfortable pension, with all the care of fatherhood and motherhood—all the comforts and many of the luxuries of a good home—while this pension was being earned. This for employees; nor has the half been told; while the city of Paris benefits to the extent of a great central hospital, and a large poor-fund which ministers blessing in every one of its twenty *Arrondissements*.

One thing brings up another, and our reference to the hospital founded by the Boucicauts reminds us of another Parisian curiosity—Pasteur's celebrated Institute for the treatment of hydrophobia. After our observations in Paris we do not wonder that inoculation against dog-bites had its origin in this city; nor that it finds here an annual quota of from two to four hundred who are needing to be operated upon. The helplessness of French femininity is something enormous, if one may judge from the vast number of females who seem to require canine assistance in getting about the streets. We were confidentially assured in London that many of the dogs in that city find an untimely destination in sausage-meat; and one almost wishes that a similar fate, or some other that would lessen their number perceptibly, might be visited upon the same species in Paris. But here they are, so far, in all varieties, and in the greatest possible profusion; and here, happily, is an effectual antidote against their bite. The number of patients treated last year was 1,559, and the deaths were four. This is a death-rate of only one-fourth per cent, which is nearly four times as good a showing as the Institute made at first, in 1886; and it is gratifying to observe that this diminution in the number of fatalities has been going on gradually with each succeeding year.

That the mind should turn toward churches after dwelling upon hospitals, dog-bites, death, and other alarming things, is only natural; and, to our thinking, the greatest curiosity among the churches of Paris is the Notre Dame des Victoires. It does not impress the Protestant very favorably that this church should have been built to commemorate the fall of La Rochelle, the great stronghold of the Huguenots. We could have wished for that conflict a different result altogether; and so, for that matter, might we reasonably wish— speaking still from a Protestant point of view—that the church itself were somewhat different. But for the devout of Paris it has wonderful attractions, and in some features it has not its like in Christendom. Beyond all other Parisian churches it is held by the Catholic mind to be, what its name indicates, the shrine of Our Lady of Victory, and the troubled in mind flock to it from feelings similar to those with which the sick and dying crowd the altar of Our Lady of Lourdes.

What adds largely to the interest attaching to this church is the fact that it is a favorite shrine of the ex-Empress Eugenie. One sees there the seven lamps she caused to be lighted in the first shock of her great trouble; and if one only knew just when to go, he might occasionally find within its precincts, closely veiled and modestly attended, that unfortunate ady herself. It is said that

Eugenie is a frequent visitor when in Paris, and that, like thousands of other devotees, she believes the shrine to have been of peculiar benefit to her. In front of the main altar of this church the light from candles is almost dazzling. These candles are lighted separately, and paid for, of course, by individuals who go there to ask special favors from the Virgin Mary, and occasionally also by those who return thanks at this famous shrine for some special deliverance. In Paris it is a proverb that whenever a person is signally favored by Providence—particularly if he should have narrowly escaped a fatal accident—he owes a big candle to Our Lady of Victory. Many are they who feel that more than a candle is due from them. This church is literally lined with memorials of gratitude. Ceilings, walls, and pillars, in every direction you look, are nothing but an endless succession of memorial slabs. If the prayer you offer for special help is answered, then you may commemorate this fact in marble, the size of your memorial to be regulated, of course, by the dimensions of your purse. This is the fashion at Notre Dame des Victoires; and it is this, with the fact of its being a repository for so many emblems placed in it by soldiers to commemorate their escape from death in the Franco-Prussian War, which makes the church an object of such supreme curiosity to all sight-seers.

You are sure to be appealed to in behalf of the poor in making your exit from one of the churches of

Paris; and in harmony with such a reminder as this, we take our readers, in search of further Parisian curiosities, to one of the quarters where large numbers of the poor eke out their subsistence. It is toward Ivry we go, the name suggesting that great battle in which the white plume of Navarre figured so prominently, and where victory for a time perched on the banners of Protestantism. But there are few plumes at Ivry now, white or otherwise. Feathers are at a discount, even in Paris, when the struggle of life is as hard as it is in this quarter. Here we see with our own eyes, for the first time, a *boucherie hippophagique*, which means a butcher's shop where horse, mule, and donkey meat is sold. There can be no mistaking this place, for it has a horse's head hung out for a sign, as all such shops have; while the butcher's shop across the way proclaims its superior grade by displaying a cow's head. There are nearly two hundred horse-meat shops in Paris, and the consumption of this sort of food last year was: Horses, 21,291; donkeys, 275; mules, 61. A local economist has estimated that horse-flesh is the staple food in one out of every three of the households of Paris. This is decidedly tough—this way of living, we mean, not necessarily the horse-flesh. That, I am sure, could hardly be any tougher than some of the American beef we have experimented upon; and, besides, the gentleman with us, who has tasted this Parisian staple, pronounces it very good.

We are also introduced in this quarter to a Rag-pickers Cité. We shudder as we glance at the rickety, one-story houses, with their dirt-floors, skirting a yard in which the pickings of the previous night are hung out to dry; and when we remember that it was only a few nights before that a Paris rag-picker, in rummaging through the city refuse, came upon the body of a woman cut up into twelve pieces, we shudder still more. Another thing to which our attention is called reminds us how very wise it was in William Shakespeare not to take much stock in names; for, as if in mockery of its poor surroundings, one of the streets here is called Rue du Chateau des Rentiers, which means, in plain English, the street of the castle of those who live on their means!

A large sugar-refinery, and a factory which turns out a favorite brand of chocolate, are prominent features in this quarter; and when you learn that the thousands of men employed in these places are turned out to support their families on the beggarly pittance of three or four francs a day, you scarcely wonder that Parisian workmen have to live on horse-flesh, or that they become furious now and then against capital and officialism. But the greatest of all the curiosities is a mammoth apartment-house—the biggest in the world, so far as our present information extends. It was built in 1869 by a philanthropist, but the aspect it wears to-day affords a striking instance of philanthropy gone to seed.

There are ten buildings connected with each other. The height is six stories; the capacity, ten thousand people; and it is stated as fact that in 1875-6 that number of Jews, exiled from Russia, were actually sheltered in this tenement at the expense of Baron Rothschild.

Its present population does not exceed two thousand; and the owner, it is said, has long abandoned all hope of keeping it clean or in decent repair. In their attitude toward philanthropy the workmen of Paris are not so complacent as their confreres in London. They regard it as an affront, rather than a kindness, and are more likely to resent than to be grateful for it. Naturally, therefore, this model tenement has been dreadfully abused. But there it stands, dignified by the charmingly suggestive name of Cité Jeanne d'Arc; and, with all its dilapidation and dirt, it is as notable in its way, and as much of a Parisian curiosity, as any of the other things we have described.

VIII.

BENEATH THE SURFACE IN PARIS.

IN asking the reader to accompany us in a tour of observation beneath the surface of Parisian life, we have no intention of leading him into the slums of poverty, nor in search of those low places, so numerous in this wicked city, where vice holds nightly carnival. Neither have we in view an investigation of that marvelous system of sewerage of which Paris so justly vaunts itself. We could not think of taking our friends beneath the surface of this city in the literal sense—not in imagination even—while the dread of cholera still impends. Besides, our quest at this time is for different things altogether, and for far better things. What we propose is a glance at some of the agencies which are working quietly for the social and moral improvement of Paris, and our reason for looking beneath the surface for agencies of this description is that, unfortunately, unless we did so we might fail to find some of them; for the aspect of Paris to the transient visitor, who has an eye only for that which is most apparent, is one of decided frivolity and worldliness. To find the better things, one must investigate and inquire. This is true in regard to almost every city; but it will be no exaggeration to say that, as applied to Paris, this discouraging axiom is more fully and more sadly true than of any other city in the world.

We should hesitate to affirm that Paris has any more downright wickedness in it than London. We question if, from the moral point of view, she would be found to be any worse than London, even when due allowance had been made for the enormous disproportion in the size of the cities. But London, spite of all its sins and shortcomings, is known everywhere as a great center of religious and reformatory work. She is as much distinguished by the effort she makes to improve her condition as by the things in her life which render such efforts necessary. That the city on the Thames is far superior to this gay city on the Seine in the latter respect would be admitted, we should think, by Frenchmen themselves. Yet even Paris has her bright side; and, as our glance beneath the surface will make abundantly clear, she is blessed with not a few heroic souls who are doing all they can for her social and moral elevation.

It will be admitted by all that the hope of a city, equally with that of a nation, is in its young men; and after seeing that the boulevards and cafés swarm with this class, and that on every hand they are surrounded by the most attractive incitements to a life of vice, we have naturally been led to inquire whether anything is being done for the young men of Paris along moral and religious lines. We have conversed with French pastors on this subject, and the information we have been able to elicit, while it is not entirely satisfactory, is at least encouraging. By one of the best authorities in Paris we have been assured that, in Protestant circles, the interest manifested in the welfare of young men is one of the most striking features of present-day evangelism. To put the matter in the very words in which our informant clothed it: "There has been more work done in behalf of young men in the ten years last past than in the forty years preceding." This was decidedly good, and it whetted our appetite for further particulars.

Inquiring next as to the forms followed by this new movement, we were gratified to learn that in individual Churches it is the fashion to band young men together into prayer-leagues, and that in many cases Christian Endeavor Societies were in operation. This reminded us of the great influence exerted upon France by that which is good in American life. French Protestantism, which is heartily committed to the Republic, has naturally a sympathetic eye for the latest advances in our own Republic, and one of the practical results of this sympathy is the importation from our side of the Atlantic of this grand Christian Endeavor idea.

Which reminds us, too, that, besides drawing moral inspiration from America, these French Reformers are frequently favored from the same source with substantial pecuniary help. Of this, one is afforded the strongest possible proof just at this time in the new and commodious premises into which the Young Men's Christian Association has recently moved. We are speaking now of the French branch of this Association. There is also, it should be said, an Anglo-American branch, which conducts its meetings in English; and this branch, in the work it does for visitors and for those who, though intending to reside here, are still imperfect in the language, can not be too highly praised. But the French branch is the one most needed, as it is also, happily, much the stronger of the two.

This enterprise has progressed in a manner which augurs great things for the future. Its former quarters had long been too circumscribed for the hundreds of young men who flock to them, and so apparent was this to a philanthropic American, when he recently visited the place, that he offered a large sum toward the purchase of suitable property adjacent to one of the boulevards. The offer was made conditionally upon a like sum being raised in Paris—a condition which was promptly met; for among the Protestants in this city are several leading bankers; and these, with others not so wealthy, came forward; in response to the generous challenge from our fellow-countryman, with a promptness and liberality which, besides being highly creditable to the individuals themselves, are especially gratifying because of the practical illustration they afford of the new interest shown by Parisians in the well-being of young men.

The many students who are attracted to Paris form

a class by themselves, and, if common report has not basely slandered them, a class which is distinguished for rather loose habits. At the present time the several faculties of law, medicine, science, literature, and pharmacy are attended by about twelve thousand; and in addition to these are the hosts of young men who are fitting themselves for an artistic career. The Paris student is easily recognized. In head-gear he will allow himself nothing more conventional than the slouch hat; and in the style in which he prefers to wear this hat, with a decided tilt on one side and an irregular depression at the top, it looks very slouchy indeed. The general run of students are cigarette fiends of the worst description; and, what is still more to be regretted, they seem to tarry long at the wine-cup, and to show a decided liking for such seductive decoctions as absinthe, to say nothing of other lamentable traits and tendencies.

Such things as these, so sadly indicative of the perils of the Paris student and of the need there is for earnest efforts to guard and save him, the visitor to this city can see constantly without the least effort. They are the bad features of the situation; and, as is customary with that which is evil, they are assertive, obtrusive, and always in evidence. Had the reader, however, gone with us one night beneath the surface—or, in other words, over to the Rue St. Jacques, in the Latin Quarter—guided by directions from those who know where to look for the better things in this big city, he would have seen and heard something of the bright side of student-life. Our destination was the office of that progressive and devout Frenchman, Pastor Monnier, and our object, to learn something of his new enterprise in behalf of young men. This is but one of several similar movements. The Catholics are busy along the same lines, and are really the pioneers in this field. But Pastor Monnier's work is a fair sample of all enterprises of this kind, and as it is a Protestant undertaking, we naturally select it for special mention.

The design is to afford cozy, well-lighted rooms in which, under Christian auspices, the students of Paris can spend their evenings; where, with the daily paper or a wholesome selection from the books provided, a cup of coffee can be enjoyed without the temptation to mingle brandy with it, or any of the other seductions of the café; and where, moreover, should inclination prompt, a game of billiards can be indulged, with no chance for gambling, and no temptation to patronize the bar. These are the main features, though, of course, there are others, some of which have in view not merely the screening of young men from temptation, but the culture of their intellectual tastes, and the development in a Christian way of the feelings and character.

In his general opinion of the life of students in Paris, Pastor Monnier could only confirm what we had heard from other sources, and had verified abundantly by our own observations. The seductiveness of Paris, he said, was enormous; and the great mass of the young men, he sadly feared, were led astray. "But there are exceptions," he observed—and we shall quite fail to do justice to this worthy man if we do not lay special stress upon this fact—"there are many noble exceptions. Most of the students who frequent our rooms are leading good and pure lives, and some of them are fervent in good works." This testimony he repeated, as though he loved to dwell upon it, and wished it to be well known; and when we asked him, as a point of curious interest, what class of students had appeared to him to furnish the largest quota of these exceptional cases, he replied without hesitation—surprising us a little, and gratifying us still more—that the most devout young men he had met, thus far, were in attendance upon the Scientific Faculty.

Here, we found, was another institution which draws a part of its support from America—a discovery which affected us somewhat differently from the one just mentioned; that is, it gratified but did not surprise us. How could it, with the knowledge we have that nearly all good causes over here are favored in precisely the same way? And naturally, in this connection, our thoughts revert to what is known as the McAll Mission. So popular is this with the best classes in the United States that we are annually helping it to the extent of between thirty and forty thousand dollars; and so much steadier is the American grip upon this work than that of the country which started it that, while the annual contributions in England are declining a little, ours show, from year to year, an unvarying increase.

The McAll Mission is another of those reformatory agencies which must be looked for beneath the surface of this great city's life. It will not welcome you at the railway station, nor parade itself before you on the boulevards, nor trumpet its doings in your ears as you lounge about the corridors of Parisian hotels. Which reminds us, by the way, that one generous American, when he came to Paris to see this Mission for himself, and was unable to learn at his hotel the precise locality of one of its halls which had been named in memory of his own daughter, became so disgusted that he withdrew his support. He had thought, no doubt, that this hall would be as well known in Paris as the Grand Opera-house or the Louvre. Yet, how could it be, when the McAll Mission is a mission to the poor—a quiet, unobtrusive evangel of gospel light and purity in a great city which, in all its surface characteristics, seems utterly given up to pleasure-seeking and display?

But this work still thrives, and we do not in the least reflect upon the native agencies operating for the same end when we declare that the doors of its modest conference-halls, always opening from the sidewalk and never higher than the ground-floor (which is wonderful in Paris), furnish a means of hope to the unchurched masses of this city, such as local effort might not have been able to present for years to come. Not in Paris alone, but in other large towns of France, is this Mission doing its gracious work; and latterly, by means of a mission-boat, called *Bon Messager*, it has begun a cruise of the beautiful rivers of France in the interest of the villages and hamlets, everywhere meeting with a warm welcome, and always, in the results it produces, justifying the view of that prefect of one of the departments, who declared: "Wherever the McAll missionaries go, fewer police are needed."

Before us, as we write, is a statistical-table of the twenty years' work of this Mission, and we note from year to year a steady increase in every department—the exhibit for 1891 being as follows: Number of stations, 136; sittings, 18,182; meetings for adults, 17,213; aggregate attendances, 991,169; children's meetings, 6,567; aggregate attendances, 297,504; total attendances at all meetings during the year, 1,288,673; visits, 29,635; Bibles, Testaments, tracts, etc., circulated, 566,635; expenses for the year, $83,015.

IX.

THE FRENCH REPUBLIC.

WE naturally look in the French Republic for analogies to our own, and some such points of similarity we find; but not nearly so many as the identity in name would encourage us to expect. Instead of calling France our sister Republic, it would be more appropriate to speak of her as a distant cousin. It is quite true that she has, as her executive head, a President; and equally true that she boasts a Senate and House which bear a close resemblance to ours. It is true also that both the President and the Legislature are creations of the people, and that they emanate, either directly or indirectly, from the broad principle of universal suffrage. The voting privilege is enjoyed in France by every male citizen who has attained his majority, the only conditions being that he shall have resided for six months before election-day in the township where he proposes to exercise this privilege, and shall not have entailed upon himself, by bankruptcy, crime, or military service, any legal disability. The last effort of the French Assembly to restrict the franchise proved decidedly disastrous. It was when, during the Presidency of Louis Napoleon, three million were excluded by extending the residential requirement to three years.

The annulling of this act was the winning card in the *coup d'état*, the sequel showing that the French people were determined to retain their voting rights, even if to do so they had to change their form of government.

Aside from the points of resemblance indicated above, the Republic of France and the Republic of the United States have in practice little real affinity with each other. They belong to the same family, but show widely divergent features. In cranial contour these sister Republics are much alike, as you also find them to be when you look at their feet, which rest in both cases upon manhood suffrage. To carry our anatomical analogy still further, we find also that they are much the same in those organs of vitality upon which the character of their legislation depends. Perhaps, too, the arms, representing the executive agencies, are very similar; for the French President does his work, just like our own, through a Cabinet of Ministers, and these are technically men of his own selection. Here, however, marked divergences begin to appear; and in pursuing the subject we soon discover that, after all, the two bodies are less distinguished for their resemblance to each other than for the many things in which they differ.

The French Republic is more nearly akin to the British Monarchy than to the form of government under which Americans live. The President is wholly irresponsible, just as the Queen is, the real governors being the members of the Cabinet. The French Cabinet, too, is entirely at the mercy of the Chamber of Deputies, and at any moment, by a vote withdrawing confidence, it can be overthrown. This is decidedly English; and just as the Queen, when one Cabinet is overthrown, is affected by such an incident only to the extent of having to set up another, so it is in theory with the President of the French Republic. Naturally, in these circumstances, French Cabinet Ministers, like their confreres in England, have a seat and voice in the legislative assemblies. In point of fact, French Ministers have privileges of this kind superior to those of the English. When Mr. Gladstone is Premier he can not speak in the Upper House, because he is only a member of the Lower House; and, similarly, Lord Salisbury, being only a member of the Upper House, can not defend his policy in the House of Commons. But members of the French Cabinet have equal rights in both Houses; and they are allowed to deliberate and speak in these bodies—though not to vote—even when it happens, as it occasionally does, that they are without *bona fide* membership in either the Senate or the Chamber of Deputies.

In the relation of French Ministers to the law-making body, the difference between that Republic and our own is as great as it could possibly be. Thus, while the American President will change his Secretaries one at a time, as circumstances may seem to demand, and will sometimes get almost to the end of his term with the staff selected at the beginning, and may do this even though his policy is opposed by both branches of Congress, the French President finds Cabinet-making one of his chief occupations. It is also a point of peculiar peril in the French system, for it occasionally happens—as it did recently with President Carnot—that the difficulty of suiting his Cabinet to the wishes and whims of a fickle Chamber will make him desperate enough to think of resigning. And this reminds us of still another difference between the two Republics. It is proverbial of our own Presidents 'that they die, but never resign; whereas, in France, resignation is the common Presidential destiny. Both of M. Carnot's immediate predecessors went out in this way; and the lesson of this coincidence would seem to be that for a country so given to change as France is, and governed as she is, a Presidential term of seven years is too long.

We are decidedly of opinion that the French Republic would gain in stability if the term of the President were reduced to four years. Every resignation produces a crisis. It shows clearly that the Constitution is not an exact fit—that it fails to work in just the way it was intended to work; and when one remembers how resignations are brought about, and that they mean usually nothing more than that the French nation is tired of the same figure-head, the argument for a shorter term becomes still stronger. France, however, though she might profitably enough follow American initiative in this matter, could hardly do so in certain other respects. To give her Presidents the veto power would be, in France, too much like a continuance of one of the worst evils of the old monarchical *régime*; and, unless all traditions were belied, it would be likely to land her before long in the arms of another emperor. The French are right in not trusting individuals with too much power. They have learned caution in such matters from long and bitter experience.

Very wise are they, also, in having excluded from eligibility to the Presidential office all members of former reigning families; and we are pleased to find that such as these, besides being ineligible for the Presidency, are debarred by the Constitution from serving as senators or deputies. The French Presidency, however, is anything but an exclusive office. In theory it is as accessible to the French citizen as the ballot-box itself. There is not even an age-limit, unless the attainment of one's majority may be so called. To be eligible for senator the French citizen must be forty, and he must be not less than twenty-five before the Chamber of Deputies can open to him; but the Presidency is within his reach, with absolutely no condition attaching to it beyond the mere formality of getting elected, the moment he is old enough to vote.

This is decidedly liberal; though whether Frenchmen are satisfied that to give them one good chance, in competition with ten millions of their fellow-citizens, to attain to the Presidency themselves is a sufficient compensation for depriving them of a direct vote in the filling of that office, is a different question. Such, however, is the situation of the case; and this is another feature in which the French Republic differs so fundamentally from our own as almost to lose all kinship with it. The French President is chosen by a National Assembly—in other words, at a joint session of the Senate and House of Deputies—the only relation of the great mass of the people to such an event being that originally, perhaps years before, they themselves elected (primarily for legislative duties) the men upon whom now the election of a head of the State devolves. If these men had been voted for in special view of a Presidential vacancy, with due announcement on their part of the Presidential candidates to whom their support would be given, the system would resemble closely our own. But nothing of this kind occurs; and it is questionable if, while the French remain as excitable as they are, our highly-approved American plan, spite of all its checks and safeguards, could with safety be introduced here.

Where Frenchmen, in the working of their political system, bear a decided resemblance to ourselves is in the tendency they have shown to pass by their strongest men, and to exalt to Presidential dignities respectable mediocrity only. Jules Grévy was a retired lawyer, his chief recommendation being that he was honest and not a meddler. The only thing which distinguished M. Carnot beyond thousands of other well-equipped Frenchmen was the great name he bore—a legacy in the second degree from one of the best men of the Revolutionary era. In this tendency the two Republics are considerably alike; but how different the reasons in the two cases! No American is big enough to imperil the Republic simply by his occupancy of the Presidential chair; whereas experience has shown that a man may do this in France even if he is not very big, but only thinks himself so, providing he has grit and the prestige of a little military fame. Because they know this, and have gained their knowledge of it in so hard a school, the French are shy of great men, and are ceasing to take much stock in great names.

This is one reason, undoubtedly, why Cabinets fall so often. Not the chief reason. That we must look for in the want of agreement and cohesiveness amongst French Republicans—in the fact that, instead of forming a great party, the friends of the Republic are divided into petty groups, who act often from motives of spite, and who, to carry their point, do not disdain alliance with the bitterest Reactionaries. Here is the chief reason why the Ministry is so often changed. The Conservatives, as they call themselves, are always against it; and when these and the extreme Radicals combine, as they frequently do, down goes the existing Government. There is, however, as we have hinted, another reason.

Beneath all this pettiness and love of change, there is no doubt a substratum of principle. Not, perhaps, the highest principle, but one certainly which has a little patriotism in it, and a very wholesome amount of prudence as well. The French are afraid of those who govern them—afraid to give them too much power, or to keep them too long in office. They have a mortal dread of despots, these late years, and are not a little apprehensive of demagogues; and surely, with the specters of Napoleon III, MacMahon, and Boulanger rising out of the recent past, there is plenty of justification for this feeling.

The salary of the French President is $120,000 a year, and he is allowed another $120,000 for expenses. Cabinet Ministers get $12,000 a year. The President, though he can not veto a bill passed by the two Chambers, has at least the constitutional right of asking those bodies to reconsider. Afterwards he has no alternative but to put into effect whatever is decreed. The style of life at the Elysée Palace is less simple than at the White House. The office of the French President is not wholly free at present from the pomp and circumstance attaching to royalty. In reference to all matters of this kind, one must make large allowance both for the traditions of the nation itself, and for her situation in the midst of powerful monarchies. The wonder is not that, with a Republican form, she still lacks in simplicity and has not yet reached in all things the Republican ideal of Government, but that she is a Republic at all.

The patronage dispensed by the President of France is trifling in comparison with that wielded by our own Executive, and in this respect the French have a decided advantage over us. All offices, excepting the highest, are non-political; and Government employees, after thirty years of service, enjoy a pension. Still the President of the French Republic has a far-reaching staff to look after. All the Prefects of Departments are under his control; and, in fact, he is represented, directly or indirectly, not only in these eighty-six larger divisions of the Republic, but in the 362 arrondissements, in the 2,871 cantons, and even in the 36,121 communes.

Which reminds us of another thing in the French Republic differentiating it from our own—namely, its tendency to centralization; or, in other words, to conserve the interests of the general Government at the expense of the local Government, sometimes even to the detriment of individual liberty. This, however, can hardly be called in truth a tendency of the Republic. It is rather a legacy from the Empire; and we may hope, therefore, that the nation, in its regenerated form, will finally outgrow it.

X.

THE LEGISLATIVE SYSTEM.

THOSE who have kept but a casual run of the history of France since her terrible defeat by Germany, may be surprised to learn that, in determining the form of the Constitution by which she is now governed, a controlling influence was exercised by the Monarchists. With their numbers so greatly reduced as they are at present, it seems almost incredible that in the General Assembly which was elected by popular vote to provide for the crisis of 1871, this party should have had a majority. Such was the fact, however; and only for the inability of those supporting the different claimants to pool their issues, the events of the last two decades might have turned out quite differently. As it was, the Monarchists, finding it impossible to agree amongst themselves, made terms temporarily with the Republicans. Not all, of course, but a sufficient number at any rate to carry through the Constitution of 1875; and one of the conditions of this memorable fusion was that the two Chambers should be retained. The Republicans were committed, both by tradition and conviction, to the one-chamber principle; but upon this point the Royalists were inexorable, and hence the legislative power was vested jointly in a Senate and a Chamber of Deputies; and one can only suppose that this two-house plan is still retained, now that the Republicans are so largely in the ascendant, because experience has shown that what was accepted at first simply as an expedient, is of practical utility, not to say necessity, in carrying on the Government.

That the French Chamber of Deputies needs some check upon it there can be no reasonable doubt. To become thoroughly convinced of this, one has only to attend a few of its sessions, or, for that matter, follow for a time the accounts one may get of them in the daily papers. A body which finds its chief amusement in discrediting Ministries, and which treats its leaders much as a child is wont to treat its playthings—setting them up merely for the purpose, as it would seem, of toppling them over again—may reflect only too well some of the traits of the French nation, but it is scarcely the sort of tribunal to be intrusted with exclusive power over the destinies of that nation.

For the facility with which he loses his head, the French deputy has no equal. This trait may be a freakish development of the law of heredity, due to the fact that in times gone by so many of his predecessors lost their heads in another way. But there he is, to whatever causes he may owe the eccentricities which have made him famous, always ready with an "Interpolation," and always prepared to follow it up, if needs be, with a duel; the embodiment of suavity at one moment, and the next an incarnation of furious hatred; loading the Ministry with compliments at one session, and by the time another convenes ready to kick it out of doors.

It would be a gross exaggeration to imply that all the deputies are of this type. There are cool heads even in France; nor can it be doubted that in the French Chamber of Deputies men may be found who, in the ability to look calmly at both sides of a question and to act like reasonable beings under the fire of ridicule or opposition, would do credit to even so solemnly respectable a body as the British House of Commons. But such men are surely not in the majority there, nor are they the men who give the Chamber its character. The average deputy, and the one most in view, is unquestionably of the type we have sketched, who is never happy unless he is out of sorts with somebody, and who always has, it would seem, not only the proverbial chip on his shoulder, but a couple of seconds dangling at his heels. The sort of scenes which disgrace Washington only about once in a quadrennium, and Westminster at still longer intervals, are of such frequent occurrence in the legislative halls of France that novelty-loving Paris has become satiated with them. We have known a single session to produce three fisticuff encounters, and to lead to as many duels, not to speak of the number of times the lie was exchanged; and though such a batch of "incidents," as the French like to call them, is somewhat in excess of the ordinary output, one may safely anticipate that if there is anything exciting on hand—like the Panama affair—scenes and incidents more or less disgraceful will be enacted every time these French legislators come together.

The Senate is a more self-contained body, as one might naturally expect it to be. The senator must have passed his fortieth year, while the age-limit for the deputy begins at twenty-five; and perhaps a further guaranty of self-control in the Upper House is afforded by the manner in which it is formed. Deputies are chosen by direct vote of the people. The electorate consists, with a few exceptions who are disqualified for various reasons, of all males over twenty-one years of age; and at a recent date the voting-lists showed a total of nearly eleven millions. All these have a vote in sending men to the Lower House; but the Senate, like our own, is elected by a different process.

Each department, or county, is represented in the Senate by from one to ten chosen men; and the choice is made by a sort of County Assembly, composed of the deputies for the county, with several county officers—like commissioners and judges—and of delegates specially elected for the purpose in the several communes or townships. This process, it is needless to say, produces a class of men somewhat superior, on the average, to those forming the Lower House. In fact, both the process and its results are similar to what they are under our own system. The Senate, however, is in no sense a privileged body; nor does it represent the classes as against the masses. It is really the creation of the people; for if these do not vote for it directly, they do have a vote in constituting the County Assemblies out of which it springs; and thus the entire system just like our own, is judiciously balanced, and at the same time thoroughly representative.

Against the 300 senators, the Chamber of Deputies opposes a membership of 584. But the senators have the advantage in length of term; for they hold their seats for nine years, while the deputies are elected for only four. In 1875, when the new Constitution went into effect, seventy of the senators were elected for life. The Chamber of Deputies had the selection of these men in the first instance; with the understanding, however, that as vacancies occurred they would be filled by the Senate itself. But this arrangement the nation has since abrogated. France has no use for life senators, and we are glad of it. She still has a few of these left; but they are dying off steadily, and the species will soon be extinct. A third of the Senate is subject to renewal at the end of every three years, consequently the Senate is never an entirely new body; and in view of the fact that the other House is subject to a complete renewal, with the chance of sweeping changes, at the end of every quadrennium, this is emphatically a wise arrangement.

The powers enjoyed by the two Chambers are equal in ordinary matters; but in the raising of supplies, or the changing of taxation in any way, the initiative rests very properly with the direct representatives of the people. By custom, too, it has come to pass that the Chamber of Deputies is the body to which the Cabinet defers. An adverse vote in the Senate is not noticed, but such action on the part of the other House is sure to be followed by Ministerial resignations. In the annual stipend allowed them, senators and deputies are on the same footing. Each man receives from the State $1,800 a year—a sum which bears no comparison with the salary paid to members of Congress in the United States, but which is at least an improvement on the English system; for there nothing is paid. Those who like to dwell upon the good side of things tell us that this payment of nine thousand francs a year brings a seat in the National Councils within reach, pecuniarily speaking, of the poorest citizen; but those who see the bad side as well as the good, think the pay wretchedly inadequate, and attribute to this fact the susceptibility of French deputies to such seductions as are held out to them, now and again, by the promoters of questionable financial schemes.

For the transaction of its business the French Congress divides itself up, at the beginning of each month, into a number of groups. This division is made by lot. In the Senate there are nine groups; in the Chamber of Deputies, eleven. Whatever may be laid upon the table is first considered in Committees of the Whole by these various groups, each group then appointing a certain number, who meet afterwards with representatives from the other groups to consider the subject as a Special Committee, the report of this Special Committee coming finally for acceptance or rejection before the Chamber itself. To be valid, every measure must be carried by a majority of all the members, not simply by a majority of those present and voting. In taking a vote, the usual method, if the subject is too important to be disposed of by a show of hands, is to cast ballots. The papers used are white and blue—the former meaning for, and the latter against. Each ballot is indorsed with the name of the deputy or senator casting it; and when the question to be decided is of great moment, the ballots, instead of being gathered up by tellers, are deposited with imposing formality in front of the Tribune.

One feature of the French legislative system strikes us as being very peculiar. We should think, however, that it would be decidedly convenient; and we wonder, now we come to think of it, that the same feature has not received formal recognition in such countries as England and the United States. We read an article recently which described, in blood-curdling language, the awful nightmares suffered by an English M. P. in consequence of the promises he had made when asking his constituency to elect him. Doubtless our American statesmen suffer occasionally from the same cause; but in France they manage things differently. Members of the French Chambers formally absolve themselves from such promises. Engagements made while his election impended are declared to be null and void when the deputy or senator takes his seat, the theory being that he is no longer accountable to his constituency, but is solely to be guided by his conscience. This means that he may not only go back on his promises to individuals, but may abrogate with equal impunity the allegiance he may have professed towards any particular principles— a liberty, by the way, which is sometimes abused, and which, unfortunately, besides affording encouragement to turncoats, prevents the development on French soil of what is to-day the greatest need of the French Republic; namely, a strong, well-disciplined party pledged to defend it against enemies and traitors.

The only occasions when the Senate and House of Deputies meet in joint-session are when, in the magnificent palace at Versailles, they take the Constitution under review, or are convoked for the equally grave purpose of electing a President. For its regular work the Senate meets in the Palais de Luxembourg, and the Chamber in the Palais Bourbon. Both places are eminently historic, and the events in which they have figured suggest in a striking manner the checkered career of the French nation. The Palais de Luxembourg was built for Marie de Medici, but received additional touches both from Napoleon I and from Louis Philippe. Before the Revolution it was occupied by the Count of Provence, who became in time Louis XVIII; and in the days of the Convention it was a State prison. The Palais Bourbon was built in 1722 for the dowager Duchess of Bourbon. Afterwards the Prince of Condé lavished upon it four million dollars; and in 1790 it was declared national property, being used at first for the sittings of the Council of Five Hundred.

Neither of these palaces has the look of picturesque dignity for which the Houses of Parliament in London are famous; and the Capitol at Washington is beyond all comparison with them. But they are plentifully adorned with statuary both on the outside and within, and, like all French buildings which antedate the Revolutionary era, they are intensely interesting. When one remembers, too, that the Palais Bourbon has twice been invaded by a mob, it seems not at all inappropriate that it should be the meeting-place of that excitable and very disorderly body, the French Chamber of Deputies.

XI.

COURTS OF LAW IN FRANCE.

THE great Bonaparte impressed himself almost as much upon the jurisprudence of France as upon the annals which teem with her military exploits. To be strictly exact, we must credit the origin of the Code Napoleon to those stormy Conventions which ruled France during the Revolutionary period. But it was under the Consulate and the first Empire that this work was completed; and, inevitably, the Code, which bears the name of this remarkable man, received from his genius its final impress of thoroughness and justice. This Code Napoleon is really a series of five codes, and with only slight modifications—these being wholly inadequate, as many think, to meet the altered conditions of French society—it has remained, spite of all changes of Government, as the supreme guide in both civil and criminal procedure down to the present day.

The appointment of judges is in the hands of the President of the Republic, who, of course, is advised in this delicate business by the Ministry of Justice. Practically the office of judge is one which terminates only when the limit of age has been reached, the incumbent retiring then upon a pension. A justice of the peace, however, may be removed at any time by the head of the State. The President can depose such a person by a word, but this power is only exercised in cases of extreme necessity; and as regards the judges of higher rank, the President can exercise the power of removal in their cases only with the consent of the Court of Cassation. This court answers somewhat to our own Supreme Courts. In ordinary law cases it has no in-initiative, its province being merely to review, for approval or rejection, the contested decisions of certain other tribunals.

Like most of the public officials of France, her judges are poorly paid. In England it is always good pay or no pay. Justices of the peace in that nation serve their country solely for the honor involved. In France the ordinary pay of such persons is about $360 a year. To skip from the lowest to the highest, the English chief-justice pockets a stipend fully equal to that of the occupant of our Presidential chair; whereas the highest judge in France, the first president of the Court of Cassation, has to support his dignity, we are assured, on a yearly salary of about $6,000. This is certainly making justice cheap enough, and it no doubt inures to the advantage of litigants in reduced costs. But it also has the effect of excluding from judicial office all who have not a private income; for it is inconceivable that high dignitaries of State can keep up appearances with no funds to draw upon save the meager salaries instanced above. One would think, too, that such ill-paid judges would be in danger of corruption; but as the French themselves are not complaining on this score, it would hardly be proper for a foreigner to do so; and perhaps, after all, the French people are as honorably served for these small expenditures as some other nations are, not excepting ourselves even, for much larger ones.

Where judges cost so little, you may naturally look for a great profusion of them, and so it is in France. Each arrondissement has its Court of First Instance; and the courts of appeal, distributed conveniently throughout the entire country, number twenty-six. The latter, for further convenience, are subdivided into as many different chambers as the particular locality may need, and each of these chambers has a judicial staff of half a dozen or so. The other courts have also a considerable staff of judges, a full bench of the Court of Cassation consisting of forty-nine. That, too, exclusive of the Outer Court, or Parquet, as it is called. This consists of the procurator-general and several advocates, who hold technically the position of assistant judges, their work being to prepare cases for trial, and afterwards to pilot them through. The Parquet is a feature of all French courts. It answers, in a measure, to our own prosecuting attorney's office, with some of the functions of a clerk of the court attached to it; but it has here a decidedly judicial standing. Not only do those belonging to it wear the judicial cap and gown, but they are ranked in legal parlance as a part of the regular magistracy.

It is a boast of the French judicial system that, excepting in the case of very trivial offenders, it allows every man a chance before at least two tribunals. This is well; but as an offset to this, we naturally recall one of the bad features of this system. This was strikingly exhibited in the earlier stages of the unfortunate Panama scandal. What we refer to is the power possessed by certain French judges to deprive men of their liberty, and subject them to rigid, not to say abusive, examinations, while it is still uncertain whether there is a good case against them. Another boast of the French is, that every case, barring only those with which justices of the peace have to deal, is tried with more than one judge on the bench. In the highest court, the Court of Cassation, there must never be less than eleven judges present. Five is the lowest number in a Court of Appeal, and for a Court of Assize or a Court of First Instance, the minimum of such functionaries is three.

The truth is that judges seem to be in greater favor in France than juries. Certainly they are more relied upon by those responsible for the French code of procedure, though they would hardly, we should think, be held preferable by those cited for trial, if one may judge from the statistics at hand. In civil cases juries are entirely unknown, and it is only in one of the courts, the Court of Assizes, that such uncertain quantities are brought into play even in the trial of criminals. But the statistics—well, they are decidedly suggestive, and they have a marked bearing on the question, often raised in America, as to whether jurymen are a help or a hindrance in the administration of justice. The figures we quote have reference to judicial procedure in France during a recent four years, and what they show is, that while acquittals before Assize Courts, with trial by jury, were twenty-seven per cent, and while of those found guilty in such courts seventy-four per cent gained a verdict of "extenuating circumstances," in the other courts, where the judges are the jury, there were only six per cent of acquittals, and but sixty-two per cent who had their punishment tempered because of mitigating circumstances.

French juries are extremely sentimental. If our memory is not at fault, it was a jury of this nationality who acquitted the murderer of his father and mother because his counsel appealed to them to have pity upon a poor orphan. At any rate, that the twelve "good men and true" often acquit over here when the verdict by right should be one of guilty, is only too apparent to even the indulgent French mind. We have not heard that French jurymen have the itching palms attributed sometimes to juries in America, but they surely have tender sensibilities, and, in some cases, rather soft heads. Beauty in distress hardly ever appeals to them in vain; and it is proverbial that in a class of cases which are rather common here—as, for instance, where, from jealousy or some other strong passion, a woman has drawn a revolver against her erstwhile lover, or perhaps thrown vitriol over him—the twelve good Frenchmen in the jury-box are almost sure to judge leniently, and as likely as not, if the woman in the case breaks down, they will not only acquit, but will do so with choked voices and with a sympathetic use of their pocket-handkerchiefs.

But there are other queer doings in French courts besides those in which sentimental juries figure. It seems strange, for instance, to find the presiding judge acting as a prosecutor. Not only does he examine and cross-examine the witnesses, but he subjects the accused to a similar process, and does not scruple to express his opinion of the latter, and even strongly to condemn him, while he is still—the verdict not having been given—presumably innocent. But this presumption of innocence does not seem to exist in France. Charles de Lesseps is told by the judge that he has been "mixed up in a dirty job," and when this opinion was volunteered, his trial had scarcely begun. This illustrates how the accused are treated; and another incident in the same trial shows how judges may comment adversely, if they choose, upon the testimony of witnesses:

The President—" Do you know who received the cash voucher for 500,000 francs?"

Witness—" No."

The President—"It is strange that you should not know. It seems to me that I myself should have been more inquisitive than that." [Laughter.]

This, though it was funny, was hardly without bias; and when, at the same sitting, this first president of the Court of Appeal interrupted another witness with the remark that if the Panama Company had never adopted the plan which he (the witness) had suggested to them, "it would have been a blessing to unfortunate subscribers, some of whom were likely to die of starvation," he not only did that which indicated a prejudgment of the case, but went so far adrift from judicial calmness as even to drag feeling into the case. But this is France, we must remember, and that is the way they do things in this country.

The French judges, however, are by no means devoid of dignity; and, excepting in great trials, when outside excitement seems to be too much for them, they are not wanting apparently in judicial repose. To make the rounds of the different courts in the Palais de Justice affords you a view of as fine a body of men as you could expect to find anywhere in France. They are hardly so solemn-looking as are their bewigged brothers over in Britain, but they appear quite too virtuous to wink at wrong; and altogether, in their black gowns and white lapels, they impress the visitor much as a body of prim-looking Church-of-England clergymen would be likely to do. They are seated on the bench in a semicircle, the president, of course, in the middle; and you notice, as you go from one court to another, that in every instance the president has before him, in a niche at the opposite end of the room, a bust of the figure of Liberty, and behind him a painting of the Crucifixion scene. Otherwise the court-rooms are much as you find them in other countries—plenty of barristers waiting for briefs, and the usual number of morbid outsiders, some of them so deeply absorbed in the proceedings that they are taking a nap.

One feature of the French judicial system deserves unstinted praise, and that is the thoughtful regard it shows for those in limited circumstances, and its really noble efforts to bring legal redress within easy reach of the humblest citizen. In regard to trivial matters, it is as much the duty of the justice of the peace in a rural town to settle differences, if he can, without allowing the contestants to come formally before the court, as it is his duty honorably to try such cases if his friendly offices are unavailing. In higher courts, the poor who find themselves obliged to invoke the law, are absolved, if they wish to be, both from counsel's fees and from court and stamp duties. Nor is this all, but almost everywhere throughout France there are special courts, made up of trade experts and of leading business men, for the settlement, without delay and with scarcely any cost, of disputes between employers and workmen, and of the disagreements occurring between rival commercial houses. These courts are a great boon, and their existence is another proof, added to many of similar import, that the France of these later decades, far from being a rich man's country, is one rather in which the workman holds sway, and whose affairs are regulated with special reference to the well-being of the masses.

XII.

THE FRENCH PRESS.

AMONG the many institutions more or less discredited by the great Panama scandal, there is not one which appears in a worse light than the French press. This medium of popular enlightenment—the guide and guard of the people, as it ought to be—is shown to have been subsidized in the interests of a mammoth fraud, by which money has been sucked in millions out of the pockets of rich and poor alike. Not only this, but it is convicted morally of levying blackmail upon the promoters of this fraud. It did more than simply receive that which was offered to it. It was not passively bribed to puff this enterprise. It was an aggressive claimant for bribes. It seems really to have been a leader in that band of social brigands who, as Charles de Lesseps so graphically put it, went at the directors with drawn poniards, and, in true highway style, demanded their money or their lives. Happily, this does not apply to all the Parisian newspapers. There were honorable exceptions. Not enough, however, to redeem the craft from disgrace, or to turn the sharp edge of censure from the French press considered as an institution.

To American thought these revelations are all the more astounding because, as it appears at present, no steps are to be taken to punish them. The papers involved pursue their career as though nothing had happened. Editors and publishers, far from feeling themselves disgraced, seem rather to be taking pride in the excellent management they displayed. We have not discovered either that there is any marked indignation toward them on the part of their deluded constituency, the great French public. Popular sentiment may change after a time, but at present it seems to look upon this latest exposé of the venality of the press with remarkable leniency—almost, in fact, with indifference. Nor is it difficult to account for this. Judged by its own recognized standards, the French press has only acted in this instance as it usually acts, and has done nothing but what is strictly proper. Speaking generally, its columns are always for sale. Between advertisements and editorial puffs the line of demarkation is very dim, and in many papers it vanishes completely out of sight.

It could hardly be said, perhaps, that it is customary for French newspapers to sell their influence to schemes of fraud; but they constantly sell it for ordinary business purposes, and many of them are bought up regularly by agents of the Government. This is no secret; and we have not heard that either the Government, the newspapers, or anybody else concerned, has any feeling of shame on the subject. As regards the papers, they openly advertise that they will publish what is sent to them, and the rates are given. The tariff in ordinary cases is from three dollars to eight dollars a line, and it is understood, of course, that what is put in at these rates will appear as ordinary reading-matter, with the tacit indorsement of the journal which publishes it. Even society and the great world of art are subsidized in this fashion. You may be quite sure that every notice you read of a wedding party, a society ball, or a theatrical performance, has been paid for at a steep rate; and as to the many disguised mercantile "ads," which the papers palm off upon the reading public, everybody understands—at least, every well-informed person in France does—that, as a rule, they will be indifferent, effusive, or superlative in their terms accordingly as the client may have approximated to these degrees in the necessary check furnished for pre-payment.

Here is a good introduction, though not a very flattering one, to a few notes upon the French press in general. By this we mean emphatically the Parisian press; for whether Paris is France in any other sense or not, it certainly is in this. Outside of this city there are scarcely any papers worth naming; and, what is more to the point, we should find few in Paris itself worth naming if we judged them by American ideals. The ordinary size is four pages, the paper used being wretchedly poor, and the appearance and make-up hardly equal to that of our average Shantytown *Gazette*. Parisian newspapers have been divided into two classes—the grave and the gay; with the *Temps* as the representative of the former, and *Figaro* as the best type of the latter. Needless to say that, in the gay capital of France, newspapers of a decidedly frivolous bent are largely in the ascendant; and it may be taken equally as a matter of course that the sort of gayety which is most predominant has a decidedly personal flavor, with not a little admixture of scandal in it.

As to the serious journals, those which make a pretense of being real newspapers and of keeping their readers in touch with current events, one can only say, judging again from the American standpoint, that the Paris newspapers who aim at this object fall woefully wide of the mark. Enterprise and freshness are two words of which they seem quite ignorant. For foreign and provincial items they depend almost entirely upon news agencies. In fact, only a few are subscribers even to these. The great mass get what little outside news they deign to publish by clippings which are often venerable with age. Not one of them has a correspondent in the United States; and when the reader only thinks that representatives of the American press are to be found in every country under the sun, and that the columns of American papers teem with European correspondence—much of it from France—he will have before him the data for a fair comparison between American newspaper enterprise and that poor apology for the real thing which goes by this name in the largest city of the European Continent.

We had thought the English papers slow enough, and everybody knows they are heavy enough, with their ponderous leading articles, their solemn regard for unimportant details, and their page after page of closely-set advertising matter. The English papers, however, do, at least, give you the news of the day. In fact, they give you a fair *resumé*, excepting from our side of the Atlantic, of the news of the world. But the Parisian press does not give anything like a fair summary of the news of France—not even of Paris. It is against its policy to do so. With these French papers news is a mere incident. The great thing is to make a sensation; and the next, to afford examples of fine writing; while another very obvious purpose is to enable scribblers to write themselves into notoriety, which they can do more easily in France than either in England or America, because, as a rule, all articles there are signed.

Perhaps, though, we ought to revise this classification, and say that French papers are run chiefly to make money, and to do this by whatever means may promise the surest and quickest returns. Speaking of advertisements in English papers, it is anything but pleasant to take up the London *Telegraph*, and find its eight pages—as we have done many times—divided off into five for advertising matter and three only for what a fellow wants to read. It is also exasperating to find long-winded editorials where you would like to see bright allusion to passing events. But in England you are never puzzled to know where the advertisements break off and the editorial opinions begin; whereas in France this is a form of perplexity which, like the poor, is with you always.

But the blame for their apparent shortcomings must not be charged exclusively upon the newspapers themselves. What we find in the press of France is only another instance of "like priest, like people." The Parisian public knows what it wants, and so evidently do Parisian editors. Some one has said that to the people of Paris an accident to a dog on the boulevards is more interesting than a European catastrophe. So it is in one sense; and they insist that their press shall tell them of such small happenings as these, not caring apparently for much beside. That the people of a city so large and so cosmopolitan should be so very narrow in their views and sympathies is one of the things that has astonished us. To the Parisian mind, not only is Paris France, but France, it would seem, is nearly all there is of the world; and it is of France, therefore, which is only another name for Paris, that they want to hear in the columns of their daily press.

And what they read must have the genuine Parisian flavor about it. That is, it must be very highly colored; must deal largely with intrigue; must mirror, in a light fashion, the gossip and movements of society; and must be interesting and piquant, even if facts have to be perverted to make it so. For what Parisians desire to have served up to them is not facts, primarily, but articles which, with just enough basis to give an air of probability to what is said, shall gratify a prurient taste, and appeal strongly to the imagination. And one can not help observing, apropos of this, that if the naked truth were more common in Parisian papers, and the nude figure less so in its art galleries and print-shops, this big city would have more to boast of than she has at present—certainly so on the score of morals.

Which reminds us, however, that salacious court proceedings are not nearly so much a feature in French newspapers as they are in English. This, because the law interposes in France to prevent such degrading publications. The testimony in divorce suits is never published. Editors and readers alike have to content themselves with the findings in such cases. In England, on the contrary, you get such slush by the wagon-full; the newspapers there, even the best of them, going to such lengths, when the law on the publication of evidence allows them, that they are called to order sometimes by even the salacious press of this city on the Seine.

Doubtless, though, it is a case of sour grapes with these Paris editors. It certainly must be; for the brightest reporters in Paris are constantly on the alert for just such "copy," barring names and dates; and it is not too much to say that matter appertaining to domestic discord and illicit affection—or at any rate having a decided trend toward such things—forms the staple of Parisian newspaper reading, whether you judge of it by the serials offered for perusal, or by the columns devoted to real or fanciful happenings in daily life.

The newspapers of Paris are in quantity altogether out of proportion to their quality. Their name is legion, and when one thinks how venomous many of them are, how spiteful in their attacks on character, and how destitute of high moral tone, it is impossible not to think of those malign agencies by whom, as a certain Good Book tells us, that name was first appropriated. But if a devilish Philistinism can ever be excused, Parisian newspaper men may surely plead a partial palliation in the fact that they hold themselves personally responsible for what they write. The trouble about duels, however, is that they kill off so few. We used to think dueling a horrible practice. Since studying it in France we are convinced that it is harmless—quite so to the participants, and to the general public a decided source of amusement. The only pity is that too often editors are treated to the safe diversion of a personal encounter when they would be more properly treated if they were hurled behind prison-bars or subjected to a heavy fine.

It is probable that most of the excesses of French journalism are due to its newly-found freedom. It was only emancipated about ten years ago, and, like the nation itself, it has come into the possession of liberty without knowing exactly how to use it. On this principle we may hope for improvement as time passes; and, of course, there are some papers even now which are as ably and as honorably conducted—with allowance for different national standards—as any *of our own. With other improvements, it is to be hoped that the poor reporter will be better remunerated. At present he works mostly on approval—that is, he gets so much a line if his copy is accepted. A newspaper reporter in Paris who gets $75 a month by legitimate means is well-off. To do this he must have several papers on his list, and, as things go now, must turn out a very spicy article of work.

XIII.

THE FRENCH PEASANTRY.

SOME of our notions about rural France will have to be revised. It has been popularly supposed that the extensive subdivision of agricultural land in this country was due, primarily, to the Revolution of a hundred years ago. There can be no doubt that the popular uprising of that period, with its political and material changes, was somewhat of a help toward this end; but that it could not have been the chief factor is shown conclusively by the single circumstance that, when the Revolution broke out, it found, amongst the twenty-five millions of the population at that period, about half as many small landowners as there are estimated to be at present in a population of thirty-eight millions. As a matter of fact peasant proprietorship, as it exists in France, is a legacy from the far-distant past. It existed and was recognized side by side with feudalism, and it has reached its present unparalleled dimensions because, since feudalism was abolished, the political and material conditions of France have become gradually more and more favorable to it.

Another notion needing to be modified is that which conceives of small proprietors as holding a larger area of the agricultural land of France than is held by proprietors of more importance. It is easy to be misled in this matter. There are portions of France, and the fairest and richest portions, of which such a conception would be unquestionably true; and the notion receives additional favor from those general statements which are afloat, like that, for instance, which puts the aggregate of landowners at eight millions, and another which states that one-half of the agricultural surface is tilled by the families to whom it belongs. When, however, we dive into figures a little, what we discover is that holdings of less than fifteen acres amount to only about a fourth of the country's surface, while those exceeding one hundred and twenty acres cover more than a third of it. We also find that holdings which range between these figures exceed considerably in the acreage they cover both the smaller and the larger estates; making it obviously true, as French statisticians have repeatedly maintained, that France, as regards the division of its land, may more properly be classed as a country of medium holdings than as a nation which is either dominated by big landlords, or cut up into piecemeal for the sole benefit of little ones.

Two other notions challenge attention, both of which will have to be changed somewhat if they are to harmonize strictly with the facts. One is the popular idea that under a system of small and medium holdings the land will be cultivated better, and hence be more fruitful, than under a different system—such a system, for instance, as that obtaining in England. In a new country like our own, where the soil has only to be tickled with the plow to smile annually with a bountiful harvest, such a result from small proprietorship might be naturally counted upon; but where the soil is old, and so nearly exhausted as to need artificial stimulus—and therefore capital and skill—to bring it into a state of even moderate fruitfulness, it is very easy to see, upon reflection, that the small, semi-impoverished owner, who must rely solely upon his own limited resources, is at a disadvantage. Not only is this what might reasonably be expected, but the figures show that it is the actual result; that, too, whether small holdings in France are compared in their productiveness with larger holdings of the same sort of land in the same country, or whether agricultural France is lumped together and compared in this matter with nations which pursue their farming under a different system.

So, likewise, must our notions as to the degree of material prosperity accruing to small proprietors be modified somewhat. Settled upon a few acres, a small family may manage to live; but if they depend solely upon what their little patch of land affords them, they will live a hard life, with scarcely any comfort, and in mean and squalid surroundings. This is the condition of a large part of the French peasantry at the present day. It is quite true that most of them lay by a little for the future; but they do this by a sort of instinct, and the reason they are able to do it is that, rather than leave the future in uncertainty, they will steal a little from present necessaries. Allowing for exceptions, we have not found that, as regards the supply of their material wants, the French peasantry, as a whole, are much, if any, better off than the farm-laborers of Great Britain. Their food is coarse in the extreme, and they are often very meanly domiciled.

The cleanliness and brightness one sees so generally in laborers' cottages in England are rare indeed in France. M. Blouet, who is surely a good authority, tells us that the average French peasant will live on eight or ten cents a day; and another writer—M. Betham-Edwards—who has traversed the entire country, says that thousands of French peasants must have seen for the first time, at the Paris Exposition of 1889, those conveniences of modern life which, in all well-regulated families, are held essential to both health and decency.

Perhaps we are laying too much stress upon these things. For fear of being misunderstood, we hasten to say that rural life in France has undergone vast improvements within twenty years, and that the trend is now more decidedly onward and upward than ever before. You can still find sections where the rude bed adorns an alcove in the kitchen; and where, as in the earliest times, horses are used to tread out the corn; as also many parts where illiteracy is common, and where the people live in the coarsest manner, and do their work without the least regard for modern improvements. But in these days education is penetrating into the most remote hamlets, and Jacques Bonhomme, under the influence of this and other civilizing forces, is beginning to think that there is more in this life, even for him, than to grub and save and then die, leaving similar conditions to his offspring. Moreover, farm wages are improving. For the lowest form of farm drudgery they have quadrupled within fifty years, the ruling rate now being from $80 to $120 a year, with board; the latter sum, which is very high for France, being the wage commanded by those "aristocrats of the farm," the shepherds. After all, too, there is hardly any pauperism in agricultural France, though there is poverty and plenty of hard scratching. And when you consider that Honest Hodge, if he lives to be very old, is very likely to end his days in the poor-house, while Jacques Bonhomme is almost certain to breathe his life away under his own roof-tree, with his own kindred about him,—it would seem as though any substantial comparison between the peasantry of France and the farm-laborers of England were quite out of the question.

That the French peasants themselves are measurably content with their lot is shown in numerous ways. One proof of it is afforded in the complacency with which they look upon governmental affairs. It is not in clustering hamlets that French revolutionists are bred, but in the close, fervid atmosphere of great cities.

Far from being a revolutionist, the French peasant is not even a politician. It used to amaze us that the popular vote, drawn so largely from this class, could change so soon from its emphatic indorsement of Napoleon III to its equally emphatic countenance of existing republican forms. On the face of it this would suggest vacillation and rural unrest; but, as a matter of fact, it indicates the opposite of all this. It shows, when one gets an inside view, that French peasants take little interest in such things, that they are wholly wrapped up in the humdrum life of the vineyard and the farm, and so absorbed in making a living and laying by a little for old age, that elections mean to them little more than acquiescence in whatever form of government may happen for the time to be in power. Anything seems to suit them politically so long as it allows them to go on quietly with their ordinary pursuits. When Napoleon asks for their support, they think of nothing beyond saying, "Yes;" and when Paris and other centers, having overthrown the Empire, ask them to indorse a Republic, the response naturally is the same. This, at least, is how it has been in the past, though one can not help thinking that twenty years of prosperous republican rule must have awakened in many of these rustic Frenchmen a pronounced liking for this simpler form of government, and that the increased enlightenment these years have brought will lead them hereafter to increased political activity.

In France, as in other nations, the complaint is common that the rural districts are undergoing a slow process of depopulation. In two respects, however, France differs in this matter from both Germany and England. We have not heard that in either of these countries there is any scarcity of births amongst the rural population—rather the contrary; whereas in France the birthrate is as low in many of the rural districts as in any of the centers of urban life, and the average of children per family no higher in some parts than in the exceptional town of Roubaix, where the last census puts it at one. Not only so, but we are assured by a writer in the *Nation* that, in many cases, "the ascertained cause of this is the desire of parents to better their own condition"—in other words, French thrift. Another point to be noted is that while the country districts of England and Germany, especially the latter, are being largely drawn upon by foreign emigration, France is suffering from this cause scarcely at all. A fact, by the way, which speaks suggestively of the superior contentment of the French.

The great drain in France is not from that country to some other, but from the rural districts toward the great cities, especially toward Paris. With increasing education there has sprung up in the rural breast a feverish desire for enlarged opportunities. It is discovered, too, that cities offer an increased wage; and, without thinking how much that is beyond price they must give up in the exchange of farm life for factory life, great numbers of the younger peasantry, infatuated with this prospect of higher pay, are gravitating yearly to the actual, and, too often, the sad realization of what it means. Unfortunately, too, the universal conscription for military service has a depleting effect upon country life—that, too, not only in the fact that it takes young men off for three years just at the time they would naturally be settling down to family life, but in the further fact that it weans them from country attachments, and makes them at home afterwards only in such scenes of bustle and pleasure as the big city offers. This is the complaint in France; and the facts to which it has reference are decidedly suggestive, showing, as they do, that in our present-day civilization city life is more than a match for country life in its power to dazzle and draw, even when farm life can offer as a special attraction the possible ownership of a small strip of land.

But as to the latter point, there are many peasants who are not land-owners. To say that one-half of the soil is cultivated by those who are proprietors of it is to say much, but not all; for the other half has yet to be accounted for. This, we find, is occupied by two classes—three-fourths of it by those paying a regular rental, and the remaining one-fourth by what are called *métayers;* that is, those who, for the privilege of farming it, halve the products they realize with its owners. To indicate still further how farming operations are carried on, it should be noted that in some cases a number of *métayers* take a holding together, bringing their combined capital to bear in the effort to make it profitable. It should also be noted that in districts where the holdings of land are generally small it is not unusual for neighbors to own a horse and a cow in jointure; and that associations are common in such districts for the purchase and hiring out of improved agricultural machinery, and for the granting, on rare occasions, of such small loans as may be needed while the impecunious peasant waits for his crops to ripen.

In social life the French peasantry are pre-eminent for the sobriety they exhibit—that, too, spite of the fact that, in some parts, their staple beverage is home-made wine. In morals they are far superior, as a rule, to city folk; so much so that an intelligent and sympathetic writer, referring to their modern tendency to imitate city folk, says that if the peasantry only knew how superior they are to the rest of France, this craze would receive an effectual quietus. In religion the French peasants are of course predominantly Roman Catholic, with, however, a fair intermingling of Protestants; and it is pleasant to know that, in most parts, the rural representatives of these two sects are on friendly terms with each other.

XIV.

FRENCH HOME-LIFE.

WE have been repeatedly reminded that the French language has no word, or even phrase, which expresses exactly what people of the English tongue mean by the word home. The nearest equivalent to it is when the Frenchman speaks of *chez moi*, which means "my house." This is suggestive; for besides lacking a suitable term to designate it, the French home—whether you judge it by American or by English standards—is deficient in several more substantial requisites. From the material point of view it is lacking somewhat in comfort. In the upper circles there is an appearance of elegance about French interiors, and a straining after effects in the matter of adornment; but there is a noticeable lack of roominess, if one may so speak, and not the attention one could desire to household conveniences. The guest-chamber is a rare appurtenance, as also are those sumptuous easy-chairs in which one can almost bury himself for a good rest. Carpets are conspicuous for their absence. Where taste and wealth are, you will find the polished floors strewn luxuriously with rugs, but in other circles you have only the bare boards to step upon. Heating is very imperfect, and a sojourn in France during chilly weather leaves you amazed at the degree of damp and cold these people can endure without appearing to be disturbed by it. Altogether the impression you get is that the French are a fine-weather and decidedly out-of-door set of people, who have yet to learn the art of a cozy indoor life, and who, paradoxical as the remark may appear, seem to be most at home when they are not at home.

Nevertheless the formalities of family life are more rigorously observed by the French than by any people we have known. There is no country where families hold together as they do here. The principle governing them in this matter is patriarchal. The home of father and mother is the center of interest for all the olive-branches, and none of these ever become so old or so fruitful as not to make it a frequent place of sojourn. Whenever it can be done, the new offshoots are prevented from shooting off literally by being still retained under the parental roof-tree; and when this is not practicable, the plan most favored is to get them settled, at marriage, in contiguous houses. We were so happy as to sit at one family table at which there were present, both then and at other times, three families. The two younger branches had domiciles within the same grounds. They lived apart, but ate regularly at the parental table; and it was a beautiful sight to see. This is often done in France. It is in harmony with the French ideal of father's home being, as long as he lives, the home of all the children.

This reminds us of another pleasing feature of French home-life—the regard shown in its arrangements for the aged. At the table above mentioned there was another elderly matron besides the venerable hostess. Who was she? Well, she was the widowed mother of a son-in-law of this family; and she was there because that home happened, at this period in her checkered life, to be the one most naturally opening to her. She was not there, however, under sufferance, but was evidently an honored guest. They attend to such things as these admirably in France. Ministers of the gospel have assured us that to find some aged dependent sharing the tender attentions of French families is a common thing, even amongst the poorest. Usually it is an aged mother—often the mothers on both sides are there. "The French are remarkable for their devotion to mother." We have heard this again and again, and we believe it. In reference to this trait, Max O'Rell, in "The Dear Neighbors," makes this striking remark: "The English assassin, on mounting the scaffold, generally gives his friends *rendezvous* in the better land, and implores his Maker's pardon. The French murderer implores the pardon of his mother."

But the family feeling in France reaches out its tendrils of sentiment far beyond either mother or father. It embraces practically the entire circle of kindred, and is almost as regardful of matrimonial connections as of blood relationship. The French have numerous *fête* days, and upon one of the uses to which they put these they are certainly to be congratulated. Such occasions are utilized for bringing together, as fully as possible, the family relations. If a meeting is not practicable, the occasion is improved by the exchange of letters. The French are great on writing to each other. This is a formality which is never omitted between either relatives or acquaintances on the 1st of January, and there are other times when it is almost as general as on New Year's day. Besides which, special emphasis is given to relationship at funerals. In proper circles, the occasion is always announced to those interested by cards; and these cards are, in one respect, a wonder to both Americans and English. You are invited to be present at the obsequies, not only by the family, but by a dozen or two of the kinsfolk of the deceased, including even cousins and aunts, and the names of all these are formally printed on the mourning-cards. What is still more touching, you find home-ties and the attachment for kindred strikingly exhibited in French cemeteries. The vaults are nearly all "family" vaults, and this fact is distinctly announced over the door of these home-like structures. Not only so, but if you visit one of these burying-places—Père la Chaise, for instance—as we did, the day after All Soul's, you will be astonished to see how generously the departed members of the family are remembered by the sorrowing portion with floral wreaths; and what will still more surprise you will be to observe, from the inscriptions upon these emblems, how many of them have been lovingly laid there by relations in the third and fourth degrees.

These are some of the good features of family life in France. There are others, of course, which are not so good; and some which, from our point of view, are decidedly bad. The smallness of French families is a standing reproach. It not only reflects on French morals, but it presents a grave problem to French economists. While England and Germany are reporting a net annual increase in their population of 500,000 or more, France is growing annually at the rate of only about 55,000, and is not unlikely, under present conditions, to become stationary. Appreciative allusion has been made to the presence of the aged in so many French homes. The fact is, you are more likely to find old people in them than young people. For vast districts of France the average of children is two in each family, and in some parts the average falls to one.

This is a delicate subject, but a most vital one. At the bottom of it you find the worst feature of the French character; namely, a calculating sordidness. The way in which they reduce the sacred function of parentage to a material basis would be amusing if it did not shock you so much. Two instances, coming under our own observation, will illustrate this. The wife of a workman, with a little boy of eight, complains mildly that, for a family of three, the apartment is too limited. "But suppose you had six children instead of one?" "O," is the innocent reply, "we could n't—we have n't room!" A lovely old French lady is visiting us, and the conversation turns upon large families. Mention is made incidentally of an honored Irish couple who increased the population of their country by fourteen. "O," exclaimed our dear old friend, "how could they afford it?" That is the French view exactly; and a few years ago the French Government, recognizing this mercenary aspect of the situation, met it in a mercenary spirit; that is, it passed a law providing that French parents, who are willing to trust Providence in this matter beyond the ordinary average of their fellow-citizens, shall be assisted in so doing by grants from the national exchequer.

French mothers, it appears, notwithstanding their fond devotion at a later period, are not at all inclined to burden themselves with the care of their offspring at the time when maternal nourishment is needed. Certainly the well-to-do are not; and hence the large requisition made upon Alsace and Brittany for those picturesquely-costumed nurses, who in bright weather, form, with their elegantly-attired charges, so conspicuous a feature of the afternoon crowds in the Champs Elysées and the Bois de Bologne. With their decided *penchant* for novelty in dress, it has also been arranged by thoughtful French mammas that the costume of these nurses shall indicate, by its predominant shades, the sex of these French babies. If red be in the ascendency, the infantile burden is a girl; if blue, the family is the richer or poorer by a son and heir. They do say, too, that for a twelvemonth or so French babies are not dressed—only swathed and bound; and that, though they are often taken out, they are wrapped up so securely against sun and atmosphere as quite to reverse in their complexions the ordinary infantile redness, and present to you instead a face that rivals the lily. This custom may account, in some measure, for the excessive mortality amongst French infants, as it may also be one of the reasons why French children, as they approach their teens—the boys especially—look so frail and delicate.

Speaking of children, however, and how they are treated in the French home, that which will seem to Americans to be more reprehensible than anything else, is the strict guardianship exercised over growing daughters, and the French notion that a young lady, to be properly reared, must be kept in almost perfect seclusion from young men. The *chaperon* is pre-eminently French, both in name and as a recognized feature of family government. Where so many women are accused of being fast, it seems very odd to think that the recognized code does not allow young ladies to go out, not even on a shopping expedition, without some older person to keep watch over them, and forbids that they shall converse with unmarried men excepting under the same restrictions. Such, however, the code is; and there are many who think that this over-zealous provision for the protection of girls becomes in the end a snare and danger to them, and is accountable largely for certain well-known aspects of French life which it would not be pleasant for us to dwell upon. That somewhat Americanized Frenchman, Max O'Rell, speaks to his compatriots very plainly on this subject. His contention is that the purity of young women can be best conserved by placing it in their own keeping. "Seeing that young people of opposite sexes are allowed to whirl round a ball-room in each other's arms, it really seems preposterous that they should not be permitted to meet together in the fields to play at lawn-tennis or croquet;" and the difficult problem of how to rear children properly will be solved in France, he says, " when our boys and girls—thanks to the liberty accorded to them from infancy—are able to frequent each other's society without astonishment."

Hospitality, in the broad sense of that term, is sadly lacking in the French home. The latch-string is always out to the children, and on formal occasions to the far-reaching circle of kindred; but the Frenchman who should wish an outsider to dine with him would be more likely to invite him to a café than to his own house. There are exceptions, of course, as our own experience has shown; but this is the rule. The dinner-parties to acquaintances and neighbors, so common and so delightful in America, are scarcely known in France; and it is also rare, excepting in the mansions of the wealthy, for visitors to be offered lodgment for the night. In large cities the flat system—which usually means an insufficiency of room—makes this almost impossible; but it is the same, we are assured, in the country, and even amongst peasants.

At marriage-feasts there is an ample spread in the peasant's cottage, and many are bidden; but beyond this the peasant's nearest neighbor, who is hardly ever more than a mile off, might as well be a hundred miles distant, we are told, so far as the exchange of hospitality is concerned. It is declared, too, that in cities you may know a man intimately for years, and may even call upon him, without ever meeting his wife or being introduced to his daughters. This is owing, as one can easily see, to those French notions, almost Oriental in their severity, which tend to keep the two sexes so much apart from each other, and which doom so many properly-behaved French women to lives of comparative seclusion.

But the French wife is not without her privileges when it comes to footing the bills. At this point, indeed, French law lays its hand upon her, and makes her a fellow-sharer with the husband in household expenses. Assuming that she has an income—as most French wives have, either from their labor or from some dowry or inheritance—assuming this, she can be held responsible to the extent of one-third of such income for whatever may be needed to support the family. This is how French law takes hold of the woman in the case. But there are many ways in which it puts the man also under bonds. In disposing of his property he can do as he pleases with only a very small portion of it. His estate, real and personal, is as much the property of his children, and, failing these, of certain other relatives, as it is his own. What is more, he can make no will which could prevent his children from being equal sharers in it. He could not do this even by a deed of gift during his life; for if he gave away more than his own "disposable quota," as it is called, the excess could be recovered by process of law. When there is one child, this quota (*quotité disponible*) is half the property; when there are two children, a third; when there are three or more, a fourth.

It seems very strange that a man should be so restricted, as all this implies, in disposing of his own property. So, also, does it seem strange that a woman in France should be required by the law to wait ten months after being divorced or widowed before she can marry again, while the man is permitted in such a case to follow the devices and desires of his own heart. But this is a strange country; at any rate, it is different from ours, and hence must be judged by somewhat different standards. We could hardly approve of all

French customs, though others of them we should be the better for copying; and it will surely appear from what we have written upon the subject that there are some most admirable and really enviable things clustering about French home-life.

XV.

THE EDUCATIONAL SYSTEM.

EVEN though there were no other improvements it could show, the Third Republic has abundantly justified its existence by the development it has effected in the educational system. Public education in France is divided into three departments—primary, secondary, and higher; and each of these has experienced within twenty years an infusion of new life, coupled with an extension of its boundaries, such as had not been known in the preceding fifty years, and which under the old order of things might not have been realized for half a century to come. Chief amongst these developments is that which has made primary education compulsory, and at the same time absolutely free. Another is the rapid multiplication of Technical Schools, which have increased at such a rate under the new impulse given to them that the twenty-six which existed in 1879 had grown in 1883 to the number of four hundred, with the most gratifying progress since that time. Then there was the establishment, in 1880, of Public Lycées for girls, which the State held to be necessary owing to the fact that the training of the womanhood of the country had been heretofore almost entirely in the hands of the Catholic Church. This, it need hardly be said, is another reform which has produced gratifying results. And, finally, there has been witnessed in France, since the Republic was re-established, a complete severance, after a brave and prolonged struggle, of the entire educational system, both in its higher and lower grades, from the domination, and even from the interference, of every form of ecclesiasticism.

There is no reason now why every one in France should not be educated, and why the poorest may not aspire after the highest educational privileges this enlightened Government is holding out. Not only is primary education gratuitous, but the training offered in the university is virtually so; and as to the intermediary stages and the schooling offered to those who wish to perfect themselves in special branches, this also is practically free to those who can not afford to pay for it. The lycées and colleges, it is true, exact a small sum for tuition and board. This is done that those having means may have the privilege of helping out the Government in the great burdens it has assumed in behalf of those not so well off in the world. It should be noted, too, that these institutions, which are classed as the agencies of Secondary Education, receive for pay pupils who would otherwise be eligible, owing to their tender age, for free tuition in the schools of the primary department. Thus all classes are provided for. Those who desire exclusiveness can have it at the minimum of cost; and what makes this arrangement one which can not be objected to by the poor is, that the same schools are open at a later period to those who pass with superior credit through the free schools. This the Government provides for by a most generous offer of scholarships; and it speaks volumes in praise of both the system and the pupils that there have been periods in which the children of the working-people, those attending the State primary schools, have profited by this offer of scholarships to the number of from 3,000 to 4,000 a year.

The conferring of degrees is a matter which the Government has gotten now entirely into its own hands. Upon this point it has had a fierce contest with the Church, but the Church has been defeated. Considering, too, that the bachelors' degree is requisite in France to admission into the professions, as well as for appointment to certain offices of State—like that of judge, for instance—it would seem as though the Government, in carrying out its motto of liberty and equality, had no other course left to it. Another fierce contest had to be waged with the Church upon the grave question of the qualifications required in teachers. Under the old system the teaching in primary schools was largely in the hands of nuns and members of Catholic brotherhoods, and all that was deemed necessary in the appointment of such teachers was that their fitness should be certified to by some bishop or lady superior. But other aspirants for places of this kind had to pass an examination, and be certificated by the State. Here was decided inequality, not to say injustice, and the Republic has cut this knot of difficulty by putting all teachers upon the same level. In fact, it has gone farther than this, and has provided that after a certain period—now nearly expired—no member of a religious order shall be employed in State schools under any circumstances.

After this statement it will be no news to say that the teaching of religion is not allowed in the public schools of France. It may, however, be something of a surprise to learn that the curricula make special provision for moral teaching, especially so when it is learned that the moral teaching afforded includes the duties owed by man to the Supreme Being. What the Government has aimed at has been merely the exclusion of dogmatic religious teaching. In other words, it has taken a firm stand against the conversion of State schools into parochial schools, and the use of public money and Government sanction—as these have been largely used heretofore—in upholding the national supremacy of a particular Church. The State is careful to declare in this matter that it is not opposed to religion itself, and it has practically demonstrated this, one would think, by the religious scope it allows in the teaching of morals. What is more, this accommodating Government has made it possible for religious instruction by the various Churches to go on, if those interested wish it to do so, concurrently with its own gratuitously imparted secular instruction. This, by providing that during one entire day of each week the State schools shall be closed, leaving the children to go elsewhere as parents, priests, or pastors may desire them to do.

Recurring to the subject of higher education, it must be noted that there is but one university for the whole of France. Strictly speaking, in fact, the University of France embraces the entire educational system, with every school controlled by the three departments before mentioned. That, however, which answers to our notion of university-teaching is carried on by what are called academies, these being divided again into various faculties. In all, there are seventeen academies, and these, of course, are conveniently distributed amongst the largest towns. Paris has one, and inevitably it is the best. This city is indeed the only place where all the faculties of instruction are represented, the other centers of higher education being variously blessed in this respect according to their importance or enterprise— some of them having only one or two of these faculties. Naturally, therefore, Paris draws upon the whole nation, and has perhaps a full one-half of all the students. To show how completely the dominant Church has been driven from its former position in university teaching we need cite only one fact, which is, that it has not a single faculty of theology under State auspices; whereas the Protestants have two—one at Paris, and the other at Montaubon. Not only so, but the Catholic Church has no properly accredited representatives amongst the sixteen hundred or more university-professors—a fact, however, which has, unfortunately, its dark side; for it is estimated by those thoroughly familiar with university life that about four out of every six of the professors are agnostics; the same authorities assuring us that the proportion of agnostics among students is still greater.

The discipline in lycées and colleges partakes naturally of that which is in vogue in well-regulated French homes. There is perhaps no country where adult life travels so generally along lines which the American would call "fast;" and, at the same time, we know of no civilized country in which boys and girls, up to a certain age, are kept under such strict surveillance. Perhaps the later excesses are a natural rebound from the earlier repression. Be this as it may, youthful life in France, whether at home or at school, is very much of a prison-life for both sexes. We are referring now particularly to high-class schools, which are largely patronized by the *bourgeois*, and where many of the pupils are received as boarders. The boys, when taken out for a walk, are always vigilantly attended, and they carry about with them a most distressing air of shyness. One is impressed, indeed, that they are altogether effeminate in their appearance, affording a complete contrast in both physique and manners to American school-boys of the same age and class. As for the poor girls, they are more demure-looking than the average nun, and when you learn what their lives are you are not surprised at this. They are watched as vigilantly at night as by day. Literally, they are never free from oversight, not even when they are asleep; for the rule in the new lycées for girls is to lodge them in long dormitories, holding thirty or more beds, these being separated only by a screen; and each dormitory has its female guard, who overlooks these sleeping innocents as rigorously, they say, as though she were a death-watch keeping vigil over condemned criminals.

As to day-scholars, they are never allowed, if they are girls, to make the distance between home and school unattended. Generally an omnibus is at their service; and if this is not used, the discipline of the school makes it imperative that they shall be accompanied there and back by some female *chaperon*—this rule being so strict that its infraction would be visited by the pupil's expulsion. There is little danger, however; for French mammas are as rigorously scrupulous in this matter as are the managers of French schools. It is, in fact, in strict harmony with the entire French system, which not only secludes girls from association before marriage with the opposite sex, but which keeps them apart until the school-life is finished, from society of every kind. The French school-girl knows nothing of parties, not even of dove parties. Such diversions are not tolerated by either parents or tutors. The school-years are years of mechanical drudgery and social abnegation; the result being, of course, that they are well educated—no doubt about that—but are as little fitted for actual contact with the struggles and temptations of such a life as is before them in France as can possibly be imagined.

To the faculties, which represent what Americans would call university-teaching, women are admitted side by side with men; and in the various professions represented, not excepting those of surgery and medicine, they are allowed in these days an equal chance with the lords of creation to practice on an unsuspecting public; but in subordinate education the sexes are taught separately. This is required by the law, and the stipulation applies almost as rigidly to primary as to secondary schools. Every Commune having more than five hundred inhabitants must have both its boys' and its girls' department—if not in separate buildings, at least in separate rooms, and with separate entrances. It is also an invariable custom for the girls to be taught by those of their own sex, and the boys the same. They are very particular in France about matters of this kind. The only variations are in maternal schools, where the children are taken before the primary schools are open to them, and in private schools, which are allowed by a special dispensation of the Government to teach the sexes together in special cases up to the age of ten. This reminds us, too, that private schools—those which are not supported, but are only inspected, by the State—cut a considerable figure in France; and most of them, as a matter of course, are maintained by the money and in the interest of the Roman Catholic Church. Over these the Government assumes control only in regard to sanitation and morals.

The compulsory school-age is from six to thirteen years. Between those periods all children must be enrolled in either a public or private school; and in case it is the wish of parents to have their children instructed at home, not only must this matter of enrollment be attended to, but after the age of eight, these pampered offsprings of fortune are liable, technically, to a yearly examination. This, to satisfy the responsible authorities that they are not growing up illiterate. When children, not otherwise provided for, are not in attendance at the State schools, the names of their parents, as an admonitory step, are placarded on the town hall; and later on, if the offense be continued, they are fined; and, as a last resort, may be imprisoned by a justice of the peace. Corporal punishment is not allowed in the schools of France; but it will interest Americans to know that one thing which is allowed in them—or, at least, over them—is the national flag. It is, in fact, more than allowed—it is required; and the reason assigned is that all public-school buildings being State buildings, they must naturally share with all other Government property the honor of floating the Tricolor.

All teachers are required to take a Normal course, or its equivalent. There are two examinations. After passing the first, the certificate obtained entitles its holder to a position only in country schools. For service in the centers of intelligence, a would-be pedagogue must have qualified in full. What makes it easier than it would otherwise be to enforce the compulsory clause in French education is, that those who attend school from six to thirteen, or who pass the standard before thirteen, are accredited to the community as having done so, the credentials they thus acquire being of great service to them in entering business life; so much so that a boy lacking this recommendation would hardly be engaged for anything but manual labor. Thus everything seems to favor the new educational movement, and that the movement itself will bring favorable returns to the Republic which has brought it to pass, can not be doubted.

XVI.

MARRIAGE CUSTOMS.

THE marriage customs of France are decidedly peculiar. To describe them intelligently we must refer, first of all, to those delightful preliminaries of wedlock which are summed up in America under the general name of courtship. At once, however, a difficulty arises; for the things embraced in that name, to American thought, are conspicuous in France by their absence. In our country we always think of courtship as something which has for its basis an intimate companionship between the two parties, and which finds its expression in quiet moonlight walks, and in the occasional monopoly of the parlor together. Somewhere, too, are American lovers brought face to face during their courtship with a great crisis. As a rule they dread this in anticipation, but it usually turns out to be anything but a dreadful ordeal in practice. What we refer to is the custom which is commonly spoken of as "popping the question." It will be noted, too, that American candidates for matrimonial felicity are referred to, in what we have said of them, as lovers, which, as a general thing, is emphatically what they are, and what a strong popular sentiment requires them to be. These are our time-honored American notions;

and they are so much enjoyed, as a rule, and seem to be so necessary to a proper adjustment of things matrimonial that we can hardly conceive how it would be possible to get along without them.

But the French manage to do so. It will seem like a singular statement, but it is only the truth to say that, in the upper and middle classes of this country, courtship, as we understand it, is almost entirely unknown. The preliminaries of wedlock are all arranged by third parties. One is spared here the happy wretchedness of falling in love, as well as the miserable delight of making a personal proposal. It would seem, indeed, as though love cut scarcely any figure in the arrangements; and as to moonlight rambles, with only the moon for a witness, young couples in France, from fear either of the man in the moon or man in the abstract, are forbidden such things. Custom, in fact, is so very strict that it does not allow them to be alone together for even a quiet *tête-à-tête* in the drawing-room. Nor is this all; but it is only under a strict system of parental oversight that the couple are permitted to correspond with each other.

One wonders how, under a system like this, the matrimonial ranks are ever recruited, and this query opens the way for some further astonishing statements. The celibate state is more common than with us. In America the presumption would be, with reference to the average young man of fair prospects in life, that after awhile he will take unto himself a better-half; whereas, in France, one would be warranted in premising, unless the young man had expressed a distinct purpose to the contrary, that he would remain single. As to girls, it would really seem as though their chance for getting married depended entirely upon how much money they have. To speak here of the matrimonial *market* is not a misnomer. There are exceptions to all rules, but these exceptions do not invalidate the rule; and the rule in France is, that a girl who is well brought up, but whose parents or friends are unable to give her a dowry, will not be troubled with an offer of marriage. She could easily enough pick up a husband from the classes she holds to be beneath her, but the caste feeling is as rigid in France as are the marriage customs; and hence our well-raised, well-educated French girl, lacking a respectable *dot*, as it is called, will presumably live on to the end of her days in single blessedness.

From this rule of exacting a dowry with his wife, one can hardly except even the humblest workman. The bride must always bring something to the union. If she is so poor as not to have a few hundred francs laid up for her wedding-day, then her *dot* will technically consist of her wardrobe, and possibly a few articles of furniture; with, perchance, a skillful pair of hands, and an understanding on both sides that she is to help out on household expenses by daily labor in some shop. And here, by the way, is a suggestion of the argument which the French offer in justification of this custom. What they say is, that amongst the poorer classes the wages of the man are so low that but for help from the other side of the house it would be impossible for the married couple to subsist; and in regard to those who are higher up in the social scale, the difficulty, they say, is the same. Young men in an ordinary way of business get scarcely enough to support themselves, and to undertake the support of another, without a proper provision for some increase of funds, would be an act of imprudent rashness; especially as French women are fond of luxury, and have such extravagant tastes in dress. This is the putting of the case from the French point of view, and it is surely plausible if not entirely satisfactory.

To this custom must be accredited a large measure of the proverbial French thrift. The advent of a girl baby into the family marks a new era in household management. This atom of humanity, if she is finally to marry, must have a *dot*, and even thus early do the thoughtful parents begin to economize and lay by in order to provide this requisite. Another effect it has on French life is to make wives, to a very large extent, partners with their husbands in business. The wife generally invests her marriage portion in this way, and, having a decided *penchant*—as nearly all French women have—for careful financiering, she generally also retains control over her investment by means of a legal partnership. In other ways the effects are less gratifying. The girl who has an ample dowry at her command, being prepared to give much, will naturally expect much in return. She will always demand the equivalent of what her own fortune amounts to; and her parents, who really have the control of this matter, will often stand out for much more. Hence she is more likely than not to find herself tied for life to a man nearly twice her own age—a sort of marriage which is hardly ever conducive to either happiness or good morals, and which in France, if all reports are true, is decidedly conducive in very many cases to the opposite of these conditions.

The effect upon young men and women is more lamentable still. Single-blessedness, if self-imposed for conscientious reasons, is a state of life which presents few dangers, and which may open to some persons extraordinary opportunities of usefulness. When, however, vast masses of young people, with no inclinations toward such a life, find themselves condemned to it by arbitary laws or rigid social customs, the results must be bad, and only bad, both for the individuals themselves and for society at large; and that results of this kind are not wanting in France is only too dreadfully apparent, whether you seek them in a certain class of statistics, or draw your estimate from what you see and hear in the large cities of this nation. But this is a topic quite too unsavory to be enlarged upon; and, besides, we have undertaken to sketch at this time, not the results of French marriage customs, but the customs themselves.

The usual course with the young man is, as we have hinted, first to make up his mind whether he will or will not get married. This question he will settle, as a rule, when he is thirty or thereabouts. Then the question arises, who are the availables, and, amongst these, which is the most promising? To settle these matters he must confer with his friends; and always one of the chief points of inquiry will relate to financial matters. The girl being found, the next thing is to become possessed of her—more particularly of her dowry. But this being purely a business matter, it must be attended to in a business-like manner. If there are parents, the arrangements are all left to them. If not, the kindly services of others must be invoked. Perhaps a priest will be induced to mediate, but more frequently still it is some middle-aged and sagacious female who acts. And now, without ever having spoken to each other except in the most casual way, the couple are engaged. In fact, it not infrequently happens that they find themselves betrothed before they have even met—in some cases before they have seen each other.

This is not a caricature—it is only a fair representation of how, in the upper and middle classes, an "engagement" is effected. What occurs afterwards may easily be inferred from what we have previously said on the subject of courting. We can only reiterate that there is no courting, either before the engagement or after it. The interchanges between the couple are purely formal, and always in the presence of third parties. After a certain probation they may embrace at their meetings and partings, but that is all; and so matters go on till the wedding-day.

Are there, then, no love-matches in France? Undoubtedly there are; because, if love laughs at locksmiths, what is to hinder him from being equally defiant toward ridiculous social customs? It may even happen occasionally that the restraints thrown about young hearts over here are a help to the tender passion rather than a hindrance; for is there not a proverb about distance lending a charm, and another one about familiarity breeding contempt? As to money being a hindrance to affection, few will suppose that a charming girl could be any less lovable simply because she was rich; or that, in a game of hearts, a good-sized bank-account would be any disadvantage to a decent man. Yes, undoubtedly, there are love-matches in France; and it is equally beyond question that many marriages here turn out happily enough. It can hardly be said, however, that the customs in vogue are favorable to such results; and one would have to be very blind, or else very kind, if he failed to conclude otherwise, after studying the matter, than that such results are far from being the invariable rule.

The only wedding ceremony recognized by French law is that performed by the civil authorities. In Paris the knot is tied at the mayoral office of one of the twenty arrondissements. Due notice must be given, and no end of legal formalities must be complied with; but the marriage itself is soon over—that is, the legal part of it; for the mayor, or his assistant, after satisfying himself that all parties are agreed, simply reads to them, from a Government book, a definition of their mutual rights and duties, and then tells them that they twain are one. In fact, this part of the business is done up in much the same style in which our American justices of the peace dispose of such cases. But usually, of course, there is a religious ceremony, and that takes longer. Those who have n't much time to spare go to Church directly from the mayor's office; but in other circles the fashion is to climb the ladder of domestic bliss by easy stages—the legal wedding one day, and the religious ceremony a day or two afterwards.

A distinct peculiarity of the invitations sent out to those whose presence is desired at French weddings is, that they are issued in the names of the parents on both sides, instead of by those of the bride only; and still another peculiarity is, that the wedding ceremony is always signalized by a collection for the poor. The basket is invariably passed, even at the mayoral office; and at church the function is quite an elaborate one. Usually it is the bridesmaids who attend to it. In anticipation of this service, they provide themselves with dainty silk bags, a perfect match for the dresses they wear; and, of course, their passage through the aisles affords a rare chance—such as no French girl could regard with indifference—to exhibit for a time, in the best possible light, their charming toilets. After all, though, the most wonderful things about French marriages are the laws which govern them, and which seem really, in their complicated and oppressive requirements, to be framed less with the object of bringing weddings to pass in a legal manner than for the purpose of preventing them. But these have been described elsewhere.

XVII.

MATTERS OF TASTE.

THERE is one respect in which the French have conquered the world. Magazine-writers may speculate as they please as to which of the modern languages is likely to become universal, but at present it is beyond dispute that the universal language of the kitchen and the *menu* is the French language. And really, with diplomacy and the stomach under their control, how selfish it seems in this people to begrudge the retention by a neighboring nation of a couple of their provinces! Especially so when they reflect how backward that nation is in those arts of the cuisine in which they themselves have so long been supreme.

One naturally expects that those who prescribe the *menu* for so many other tables, will not be neglectful of their own, and that such a people, being unrivaled adepts in cooking, are not unlikely to be over-indulgent toward themselves in the matter of eating. This was the writer's expectation; and his experiences and observations in France have not only justified it, but have revealed a picture of gastronomic predilection which exceeds even that which his fancy had previously painted for him. It must surely be that the French, far from merely eating to live, are a people who afford the best modern example of what it means to live merely for the sake of eating. The way they begin in the morning is no criterion whatever of how they will finish up at night. They treat the table in the early hours of the day much as a cat treats a new conquest from the kingdom of mousedom. They are sure of it for final indulgence, and hence they begin by affecting toward it a sort of disdain. For the first breakfast, coffee and rolls will suffice. This is the play to which the mouse is treated as a preliminary to the more tragical performance. It is one of the deceiving ways these French have, by which the visitor, if he judged too hastily, might be seriously misled in regard to them.

Another deceiving thing about the French treatment of the table is the rarity of their formal approaches to it, and the long waits between times. In England you can be quite sure of four meals a day, and in Germany you will be lucky to get off with less than five or six; whereas, in France, the daily assaults of a formal kind number only two—the *déjeuner*, or second breakfast, which occurs at twelve or one, and the dinner to which you sit down in state at six or seven. Of course, you will have begun the day with the inevitable coffee, and may have had tea—*à l'Anglaise*—in the afternoon. But what you get on these occasions will not inconvenience you in the least, and your serious dependence will be upon the two meals mentioned above. And what feasts these will be! For the variety afforded, and for the time consumed in doing justice to them, to say nothing of the mystery attaching to some of the dishes, the visitor will never have known the like before, unless, perchance, it shall have happened that he has been in France before. As to the French themselves, the amount of execution they manage to do at these two formal assaults upon the dining-table is almost incredible. As regards the upper and middle classes, the richly-cooked meat they dispose of is far in excess of the daily consumption by the same classes in America; and that means that England and Germany are so far behind as to be out of the race altogether.

Apropos of this, a very discriminating writer, and one who is inclined to extenuate French foibles rather than to set down aught in malice, has said:

"English writers are often on the lookout for subjects of accusation against the French, and they generally hit upon immorality. May I give them a hint that may be of use, at least, in affording the refreshment of change? Why do they not accuse the French of gormandism? There are a hundred proofs of that vice for one of the other. It is visible everywhere in France, and in some parts of the country it predominates over all other pleasures of life. Most well-to-do French people, who live in the rural districts and are excessively dull, find a solace and an interest twice a day in the prolonged enjoyments of the table. There is no country in the world where so much thought and care, and so much intelligence, are devoted to feeding as in France."

All this we fully indorse, barring, perhaps, that allusion in the paragraph which seems to discredit the popular estimate of French immorality. We sympathize, too, with the general conclusion announced by this writer. The author we are quoting is P. G. Hamerton, who has written an able work on "French and English." Luxury in food and dress, he says, are two great parent evils in France; and he does not hesitate to contend that the passion for good living is one of the things which tends to keep down the birth-rate in France. This, because by adding so enormously to household expenses, the tendency in question makes it an object with heads of families not to have too many mouths to fill.

To illustrate the playful, mincing way in which the French begin their daily exercises in gastronomy, in contrast with the way in which they continue and end them, the old figure of the cat and the mouse was employed. This figure we have a special reason for recalling. Besides illustrating *how* the French eat, it is not without its suggestiveness as to *what* they eat. Mice? No; not that we are aware of. But, unless they are shamefully belied, they serve up some dishes compared to which mice—pickled, stewed, or done up in hash—would be an appetizing dainty. This reminds us of another of the deceiving ways of the French—that of cooking things in such an artful manner as completely to disguise them.

"Your French *chef*," it has been well said, "will take a piece of old horse or fusty beef, and make a *ragout* that will cause you to smack your lips and cry for more. He will so dress you a stale fish that you shall imagine you are eating the most delicious *plat*. He will give you stewed goat so disguised that he might safely wager his head to yours that you would not tell the dish from jugged hare. He will give you tripe, and make you believe that you are eating fish; and fish, and you shall think you are partaking of game." But it was neither fish nor game of which Mrs. Fred Burnaby and her companion found themselves partaking; and the disguise, moreover, was so incomplete, for a wonder, that these happy Englishwomen were able to penetrate it. The lady first mentioned vouches for this instance in her book, "The High Alps in Winter." She and her friend were dining at a French hotel. Suddenly the companion dropped her knife and fork, and exclaimed: "I know what this dish is—it is slugs!" And slugs it was, as the two ladies fully convinced themselves, both by further scrutiny and by subsequent inquiry.

It must not be thought, however, that such dishes as these form the staples of French eating, or that they are indulged in to any considerable extent. They are rather the dainties of the French *menu*, which you would scarcely get excepting in the highest circles, and there only as an occasional relish. The staples, in good society, are good meat and good potatoes—cooked, however, in all conceivable ways, and in some ways which, to the ordinary mind, must be antecedently inconceivable. As to workmen and those still poorer, such classes live in France as they do elsewhere; that is, they eat what they can get, and it goes without saying that their principal reliance is that catch-all of the French kitchen— the soup-bowl.

From French tastes in eating we pass, by a natural transition, to French habits in drinking. Public drinking in France is very public indeed. The drinking-places stretch so far across the sidewalks as to be almost as much out of doors as in. There is hardly anything the average Frenchman enjoys so much as to sit with a boon companion in front of a Parisian café, and thus, as he watches the crowd go by, put in public evidence his bibulous propensities. We have mentioned the café because it is the best representative of its class; but the drinking-places of France have a variety of names. There is the buvette, the cabaret, the guingette, the estaminet, the brasserie, and no doubt others whose names we have yet to learn. It is said that the average of such places, for the whole country, is one to every eighty-eight inhabitants. Not much danger of anybody going thirsty.

The chief indulgence is in wine, which is very cheap

even yet, though not so much so as formerly, and which must also be decidedly weak, judging from the quantity people can consume without showing the effects of it. For the average Frenchman, in good circumstances, the consumption per day is about two bottles; and many, as night draws on, take in addition to this a considerable quantity of stronger stimulants. For the average woman, in the same situation in life, the daily consumption is less. We have seen it seriously stated that those ladies who are especially moderate in their indulgence, confine themselves to half a bottle of red wine at each of the two principal meals. But the same writer assures us that, during years of observation, he has never seen an intoxicated woman in this country; and it is the universal testimony, both of the French themselves and of foreign visitors, that French women, while they are rarely total abstainers, are still almost entirely free from the vice of drunkenness. In this respect, the lower classes of French femininity afford a contrast to the same classes in England which can only be appreciated fully by those who have seen it for themselves.

France has always been regarded as the country *par excellence* of moderate drinking; but in the book previously quoted from, Mr. Hamerton speaks of it as a country where moderate drinking is carried on to an extent which makes it really immoderate. We like to quote this author because, though writing for the English, he speaks always with marked fairness, and, if anything, shows a bias in favor of the French.

"Men are called moderate drinkers," he says, "so long as they do not show any outward sign of being 'the worse for liquor.' But there is an education of the body by which it may be made to absorb great quantities of alcoholic stimulants without exhibiting anything in the nature of drunkenness. In France it is considered shameful and disgusting to be drunk; but no blame is attached to the utmost indulgence in drinking so long as it keeps on the safe side. This leads to that artful kind of drinking which is well known to all French physicians, and which produces, in the long run, that peculiar state of body which they call '*l'alcoolisme des gens du monde.*' A peasant may get perfectly drunk once a month, and yet be a very small consumer of alcohol; a gentleman, without ever being even tipsy, may consume five times as much alcohol as the peasant."

We have spoken of the French as inclining chiefly, in their bibulous propensities, toward the wine-bottle. This they do, though latterly they have developed quite a liking for the beer-keg; and, what is still more unfortunate, for the whisky-jug and the brandy-flask. In some districts these tendencies are decidedly striking. Statistics show that the largest consumers of beer are in the towns of Lille, Roubaix, Tourcoing, St. Quentin, and Amiens, where the yearly average consumption ranges from forty-five to sixty-seven gallons per head of the population; whereas, in Paris, the average is less than three gallons per head. The consumption of alcohol is greatest in Normandy and Brittany, attaining nearly four gallons per head in Rouen, Havre, and Caen; while it is over two and a half gallons per head at Brest (Brittany), and nearly two gallons per head in Paris.

One reason why wine is less indulged in than formerly is because, since the visitation of phylloxera, it has increased somewhat in price, besides having deteriorated in quality. The yield even now, after many years of partial recovery, is less than it used to be by fifty per cent. France does not produce at present nearly enough wine for her own consumption, though the yield last year approximated to six hundred and sixty million gallons. Those who have thought that she supplied the world with this liquid, will be surprised to read that her imports for eleven months of 1892 were two hundred and four million gallons, and her exports only thirty-nine millions.

From these figures it will be seen that the French still drink wine in anything but moderation. To show, however, how the increase in the price of this beverage has affected their habits as regards stronger liquids, we quote again from P. G. Hamerton, who says: "The effect of dear wine in France has not been favorable to temperance, but the contrary, by increasing the consumption of poisonous spirituous liquors. That has now reached such a pitch in the working-classes that drunkenness of the most dangerous kind—the kind unknown in wine countries—is established amongst them as it is in the lower orders of London or Glasgow. In fact, the worst form of Scotch dram-drinking is common in the great French cities."

The same observer feels quite sure that while the drinking habits of the English and Scotch are improving, those of the French are, on the whole, getting worse; and statistics seem to prove this. As to drunkenness, one sees comparatively few cases on the streets, excepting in the very lowest districts; but the police courts tell a tale the significance of which is as deplorable as it is unmistakable. It was not until some time in the seventies that the nation felt called upon to take judicial notice of this offense. When one observes, however, in the police statistics for a recent four years, that the annual average of arrests for drunkenness in the whole country amounted to about one hundred and nineteen thousand, a glimpse is afforded of the trend of things in France which is anything but pleasant, and which promises sadly for the future.

The prevalence in France of the absinthe habit, and of the liking for such decoctions as *eau de vie*—drinks which are destructive to the nervous system, and which lead often to paralysis and madness—this we have found to be not only as general as we had been led to expect, but even more so. You can recognize absinthe by its whitish and foamy appearance, and the frequency with which we have observed it in front of young men at the outer tables of French cafés has surprised and shocked us. Akin to this is the French habit of grading their drinks according to strength and quality, with special reference to the time of day. Upon this habit, Mr. Hamerton, who is by no means an apostle of temperance as we understand it, makes the following observations:

"The most insidious form of French drinking is that which provides a varied succession of stimulants, in methodical order, with not very long intervals—an arrangement quite as regular as that of prayers in a monastic establishment. It is, in short, a systematic organization of Bacchus worship, combining the most faithful observances with a decent external prudence. There is something extremely French in this; for of all peoples the French are the most ingenious in making programs of successive pleasures, to come each in its due time."

We have read several authorities on the drinking habits of the French, and most of these have given what they are pleased to call a fair view of the temperance side of the question. These writers, however, have treated of temperance as if it meant nothing more than moderation. There are many in France, they tell us, who drink wine only with their meals, and many who seldom, or never, visit a public drinking-place. These are presented to us as the temperance folk of this nation, and one might easily suppose that there were no others holding up this banner. But the writer has made a gratifying discovery. He has found in France a *real* temperance element—an organization of total abstainers. Its headquarters are in Paris. Its honorary president is Leon Say, a senator and distinguished economist; its acting president, Pasteur Monnier, who is referred to elsewhere as a leading worker in behalf of Paris students.

Here is real hope, but how small and feeble its beginnings! The Society of the Blue Cross, as it is called, enrolls throughout all France from 1,500 to 2,000 adherents. In gathering these it has been at work since 1885. In Paris it has a membership of 500. These are the statistics, and, standing alone, they are somewhat disheartening. When, however, you meet the workers, and learn a little of their methods and of the present status of things, you feel differently. In Paris the work is carried on by ten sections. In each section a representative meeting is held monthly, at each of which from six to fifteen persons take the pledge. Half of the 500 in Paris have been enrolled during the present year. That shows a rapidly growing interest. It indicates present-day vitality; and the round one hundred of accessions, within the same length of time, at Rouen, is another indication of the same kind. Other provincial towns which are making good reports are Lyons and Marseilles, though the greatest progress of all is being made among workmen in *Pays de Mont-beliard*. Thus the cause of temperance is making some progress even in France; and we can only wish, scarcely daring to expect, that the good work of the Blue Cross, of the World's Woman's Christian Temperance Union, and of any other struggling organizations which have a foothold there, may increase and abound in that country in the same way in which such work has long done in our own Nation, and is now doing in Great Britain.

XVIII.

CHURCH AND STATE.

IN the contest for supremacy between the Catholic Church and the French Government, the event of greatest importance within recent years was the Encyclical of Pope Leo XIII, which summoned Catholics, both lay and clerical, to a cordial support of the Republic. Previously the Church, as every one could see, was a decided enemy of the Republic. Its hierarchy, its religious communities, even its priesthood—with rare exceptions—were opposed to existing forms, and either openly or secretly were planning and praying for their overthrow. The alleged cause of this hostility to the Government on the part of the Church was the antipathy which the Government had shown to the aims and methods of Roman Catholicism. The Government, however, could just as reasonably allege a similar excuse for its own attitude, and, as it appears to us, had far more facts at hand to justify such an excuse; for the aggressors in this warfare were not the upholders of republicanism, but the agents of Romanism. From the moment of its establishment it was evident to all that the Republic could expect no support from the Church; and what was thus a foregone certainty, thoroughly understood by all parties in 1872, has been abundantly corroborated by subsequent events. The only variation has been toward increased bitterness. This Church has not been content to fare as other denominations have done. It has demanded ascendency; and because the Republic would not grant this, but was determined that all religions should be on an equal footing, and that none of them should be used for political purposes to the injury of the State, the Catholic Church in France had remained the friend of monarchy and the foe of republicanism, tolerating the latter only as an unavoidable evil, and always hoping—to put the case as mildly as possible—for the re-establishment of the former, up to the very moment when, like a herald of peace out of a stormy sky, Pope Leo's famous Encyclical was put forth.

In the year or more which has elapsed since that occurrence there has been a change. The pope's action has mollified, in some measure, both parties to this controversy. It was only natural that the Government should be pleased, for the French Republic is none too strong. Certainly it is not strong enough to look with indifference upon the attitude toward it of a Church which embraces nominally all but a small minority of its citizens. Not only is the Government pleased, but in various ways—notably by friendly actions toward the pope on the part of M. Carnot—it has given expression to its pleasure. It is easy to discover, also, that a gradual change is occurring in the Church. It is no doubt true that the hierarchy of France, supported by titled laymen, have sought by protests and arguments to produce at Rome a recantation of the late edict. But where popes are concerned it is usually the other fellows who have to do the recanting, and so, evidently, it will have to be in the present instance; for his holiness stands so firmly by his guns that he can not be intimidated by even the Panama disclosures—his reply to those who have urged these as a pretext for the withdrawal of his support being, "That the scandals in France condemn the guilty persons alone, and not the Republic;" and that, furthermore, "it ought to be the mission of French Catholics, for the welfare of France and of religion, to get rid of all the public men who have had a share in these scandals."

Perhaps, if the truth were known, the French Government is more pleased with the altered attitude of Rome than French Catholics are. The change in the Church is very slight so far. Such leaven will make its way in so obstinate a lump very slowly. Even a papal encyclical can not work a miracle. The element to be chiefly reckoned with is the aristocracy. These are essentially Royalists almost to a man, and they are attached with equal unanimity and heartiness to the Catholic Church. It is hardly conceivable that a papal edict will transform into partisans of the Republic such stanch supporters of monarchy as the French nobility have always been; and it remains to be seen whether their influence, with other causes to help it, may not be more potent in the long run than that of Rome itself.

As to the motives of Pope Leo, we can only speculate upon them. It is thought in Italy that his course in this matter is a bid for French help in recovering his long lost and still lamented temporal power. In France the fear of Protestants is that he is seeking the reconciliation of the Church to the Republic for the final object of converting the Republic to the Church. Others, however, hold to the milder view that he wishes to free the Church from the odium of political conspiracy, and would place her in a position of friendliness toward the Government in order that she may the better carry on her work, and may be more likely than she has heretofore been to have a fair share in any favors the Government may have to disburse. Accepting as correct the last of these views, it is impossible to see in the pontiff's action anything inimical to good sense, or contrary to good morals; for, as things have gone in France these twenty years past, the Catholic Church has been at a decided disadvantage in that country; so much so that, in spite of her vast preponderance socially and numerically, she has not wielded as much power in governmental affairs as either Protestants or Freethinkers have done.

To admit this is a different thing altogether from conceding that the French Republic has gone to the length of persecuting this Church. Such a charge we hold to be purely gratuitous. Whatever martyrdom the Catholics have suffered has been voluntary on their part. Not only so, but it is largely a matter of the imagination. In compelling the Jesuits to disband, the present Government has only done what had been previously found necessary by even the Bourbons; and, in fact, the measure of 1880 was less severe than that of 1762. It was during the fierce passions of the Revolution, not under the mild sway of the Third Republic, that Church lands were sold for the benefit of the State. The Republic, on the contrary, has sought, according to Bonaparte's plan, to make amends for this act of pillage by continuing regularly its annual grants to the Catholic clergy. As to English criticisms upon this subject, the point is well made by Mr. Hamerton, in "French and English," that in confiscating property which belonged to the Church these two countries are alike—the only difference being that England gave nothing to the Catholics in return; whereas France guaranteed to them, and has continued to pay, a large annual interest on what was taken.

Not a few of the acts of hostility with which the French Government is charged are in reality municipal measures. It was Paris, through its radical Council—not the Republic—which tore the crosses from the gates of public cemeteries in that city; and to the same initiative, more than to any other, is due the exclusion of so many nuns from service in municipal hospitals. In calling to order a certain class of unauthorized religious brotherhoods, the Government of France has simply acted in self-defense. It became convinced that they were agencies for the spread of sedition against its own life; that they were drawing off from the tax-list and from army service more men and more money than could be safely spared; and, what was still worse, that they were hoarding wealth to be used as occasion offered in pampering Boulangist demagogues, and furthering the schemes of worthless Royalists. If this conviction was a mistaken one, why did not these orders take advantage of the opportunity which was given them to prove their innocence? In other words, why did they not apply for an "authorization," and demonstrate, if they could, their right to the same consideration which was accorded, and which is still accorded, to what are known as the "authorized" brotherhoods, and to the numerous retreats throughout France into which Catholic women retire? Instead of this, they pose before the world as martyrs. In reality they are not killed by the Government; but they commit suicide, and thus virtually plead guilty.

Another act of self-defense to which the Government has been driven is that which, after a certain date, will exclude members of religious orders from serving as teachers in State schools. This was long delayed; and the reason so extreme a measure was finally passed was that the Catholic Church, and especially the religious brotherhoods of that Church, were the avowed enemies of the public-school system. They were notoriously out of touch with what the Republic held to be vital—namely, liberty of conscience; and hence could not be trusted to administer fairly a scheme of education which was intended to maintain that liberty. The Government has never said that they may not establish schools of their own, and it offers no interference with what they may choose to teach in such schools. They are still at perfect liberty to educate their own clergy; and if they were able, from a financial point of view, they might maintain parochial schools enough for the education of all Catholic children. In this matter they have the same rights which all others enjoy in France. The Republic, however, is determined that they shall not control its State schools, nor use them as recruiting-offices for their own Church.

It would seem, in one view of the case, as though the charge of being opposed to religion were the last which could be laid with truth at the door of the Republic of France; for it supports, by large annual grants, no less than four religions. It is decidedly impartial in this matter, and somewhat inconsistent perhaps; for, as a critical writer points out, it pays Catholics for affirming the Real Presence, and Protestants for denying it; Christians for holding that Christ is God, and Jews for scouting this doctrine; while in Algeria it upholds Mohammedans in maintaining that the representatives of all three of those religions are infidels. Besides showing its impartiality in this way, it gives further proof of it by holding all these Churches or creeds subject to the same general laws.

The trusteeship of Church property rests in the Central Government; and on the Local Board, which controls it, the mayor sits side by side with the priest or pastor, both being members *ex officio*. Changes in discipline are subject to governmental sanction; as also, in all the Churches, are the appointment and removal of most of the ministers. In addition to all this, situations are possible in which the affairs of State-aided Churches may be brought for adjustment before a special Court of Appeal; and, what is still more, the Republic can at any time, by a simple majority in the Chamber of Deputies, cut off supplies. That is, it could refuse to vote the annual budget from which the clergy of these State-aided religions derive most of their support. These are some of the means by which the Republic of France, in return for the help it gives to these Churches, exercises supervision and discipline over them.

At a recent period the Catholics of France were returned at 980 per 1,000 of the population, and the Protestants at 16 per 1,000; the remainder being distributed amongst various other beliefs. The annual budget for the support of Catholic worship amounts to from $8,000,000 to $10,000,000, while the Protestants receive annually about $350,000, the Jews about $40,000, and the Mohammedans about $50,000. It has often surprised us that a nation so predominantly Catholic as France could oppose so successfully the encroachments of that Church; and especially that, while acknowledging a formal adherence to it, it could come, as it evidently has in these latter days, to dislike and distrust it so thoroughly. To our thought, there is something suggestive in such a situation, and the implication it conveys is not a flattering one. It would seem to indicate that those who have waited upon Catholic ministrations have not been favorably impressed by them, and that the Romish system, as France has known it, has failed to inspire popular confidence.

Not only so, but upon the testimony of competent judges, this Church has failed sadly as a religious force. M. Betham-Edwards says, in "France of To-day:" "We can not shrink from a conclusion forced upon us by accumulated experience. The only spiritualizing influence hitherto within the peasant's reach has failed to touch him. We gladly acknowledge his high qualities, probity, thrift, respect for authority, self-denial. For higher things we must not always look. Yet we have here the offspring of that Church which has nowhere ruled with more powerful sway."

In a critical work on "France as it Is," written by two Frenchmen—André Lebon and Paul Pelet—the question, "Is France a religious country?" is answered thus: "It is very difficult to give a positive reply to this question. Talk with individual Frenchmen of any class, and we shall almost always find—with the exception of the province of Brittany, where faith is strongly rooted—a skepticism readily passing into mockery, and bordering on indifference, on the subject of religion. On the other hand, any one who enters a church or religious temple at the hours of service will generally find them filled with worshipers. Ask a peasant his feelings towards his priest, and he will show a certain inveterate distrust of the priestly garb; but the same peasant will be married and buried by the Church, and will have his children baptized and confirmed. Finally, a general view of contemporary French history will show that there are few countries where the struggle between the civil power and religious authority has been more constant; few in which—first the liberal, then the democratic, movement has had a more anti-religious tendency; few where greater contradiction is to be met with between the external habits of the citizens and the slow and continuous mental cleavage which has come about between them and the Church. This complex situation arises from the fact that the religious question has been constantly entangled in the present century with political questions, and that most civil and social reforms have been carried out at the expense and despite the opposition of the Catholic Church."

XIX.

FRENCH PROTESTANTISM.

STATISTICS show that in round numbers the Protestant Churches of France enroll a membership of about 600,000, and that about 500,000 of these are embraced in the old Huguenot or Reformed Church. This, and the Lutheran Church, are the two Protestant bodies which receive aid, and, with it, more or less of supervision and moral countenance, from the State. Other Protestant sects, however, have a good foothold in that country, and are equally free, with Reformers and Lutherans, subject to the general law, to carry on their work of evangelism. With the exception of the greater influence possessed by the latter in consequence of its preponderating numbers and superior social position, Protestantism is on the same level under the Republic as Catholicism. We have heard of a curé who spoke condescendingly to a Protestant clergyman of "the tolerance" manifested toward Protestantism. But the proud and truthful retort was: "There is no longer any question of religious tolerance in France; one and all, in the eyes of the law, stand precisely on the same footing." Among the Protestant agencies which manage to get along very well without aid from the State are the Free Church, the Baptists, the Wesleyans, and last, though by no means least as an evangelizing force among the masses, the McAll Mission.

The influence wielded by French Protestantism is largely in excess of its numerical strength. It is not without its representatives in banking circles, and in the provinces it cuts something of a figure in the highest social circles, while in governmental affairs it takes a rank which is surprising. There was a National Cabinet not long ago, which embraced five men who were nominally Protestants. M. de Freycinet, who took the war-office after Boulanger, the first civilian who ever occupied this post, and who held it for six years, is of this number, and his wife, we are told, is an active Protestant worker. In diplomacy the Protestants lay claim, by family descent, to M. Waddington, long the distingushed representative of France at the Court of Great Britain. Leon Say, a distinguished economist, and one of the most influential members of the Chamber of Deputies, is a Protestant. So likewise is M. Brisson, who has acted with so much spirit as chairman of the Panama Commission of Inquiry. To these must be added the dean of the Paris Faculty of Letters, Rabier, Director of Secondary Instruction, and Monod, Director of Assistance Publique; while in the French Institute, the Protestant names of Dumas, Ph. Berger, and Appell stand out to greet us. These, moreover, are but a few of the more distinguished in this honored galaxy.

As to the relative influence of Catholicism and Protestantism in political circles, an American priest, who had been two years in Paris, expressed to us the indignant conviction that the latter was "a thousand times" more potential in that sphere than the former. This, of course, was an exaggeration, though, perhaps, a pardonable one. Certain it is, at any rate, that the Protestants have more influence, far more, than the Catholics have, in proportion to their numbers. At Toulouse, some time ago, M. Carnot, in receiving a deputation of Protestant clergymen, alluded, we are told, not only " to the respect but the affection " with which their Church was regarded by the Republic ; and, assuming this affection really to exist, it is not difficult to account for it; for Protestantism has never asked for ascendency or for special favors of any kind. It has sought only liberty and equality, and the Third Republic has ample reason for both respecting and loving it, in the simple fact that it has constantly upheld republican institutions.

By a Protestant pastor in Paris we were afforded a view of a French map, showing the location of Protestant churches in that country. From this it became distressingly evident that there are immense districts in France where that Church has no representation. Even the birthplace of Calvin is suffering from a deprivation of this kind. When, too, we observed that the chief strength of Protestantism is in the neighborhood of certain seaports, and in territory near to the frontier, we could not help thinking that we had before us a pathetic object-lesson, which indicated only too plainly the checkered and bloody history of French Protestantism. What this means is, that after the revocation of the Edict of Nantes, those who remained true to their faith either fled the country or migrated to places from which a flight on short notice would be convenient. Thus it is that Protestants are found in greatest number even to this day in the departments of Drôme, Doubs, Deux-Sèvres, Ardèche, Lozère, and Gard; and to give an idea how they stand in at least one of these counties, we quote from M. Betham-Edwards, in "France of To-day:"

"The department of the Gard offers an anomaly pleasing to English observers and progressists generally. Here, and here alone throughout the length and breadth of France, are found villages without a Catholic Church, villages that have held fast to Protestantism and the right of private judgment from time immemorial. Nor is it among the meek and the lowly that the more enlightened doctrine has chiefly prevailed.

"In higher places the Protestant element is overwhelming. Alike moral and material, spiritual and intellectual forces are here arrayed against intolerance and superstition. Were the same spectacle witnessed elsewhere, and the Gard no phenomenon on the French map, we might draw good augury for the future. Half a dozen departments Protestant to the core, and Boulangisme were impossible, Lourdes a survival to blush at, the cloistered convent out of date as an *auto-da-fé*, France saved by the remnant. We must be thankful to find one such department out of the eighty-six.

"That this tremendous Protestant supremacy should excite concern and disquietude in the opposite camp need not surprise us. A Nimois Catholic, recently writing to the Ultramontane organ, *L'Univers*, pointed out that the three senators then representing the Gard (1891) were all Protestants. At the general elections of 1889, out of six Republican candidates, five were Protestants; of the six deputies who sat in the Chamber, five were Protestants, the sixth being a Jew."

With reference to the same department, a correspondent of the London *Daily News* says:

"The County Council of the year (1891) is made up of twenty-three Protestants and seventeen Catholics. The seven members of the Board of Hospitals at Nimes are all Protestants; three out of the four inspectors of health are Protestants, as well as the four chairmen of the Councils of Hygiene in the four departmental districts. Nine out of the twelve head-mistresses of the public schools for girls belong to the Reformed faith; the Chamber of Commerce numbers eleven Protestant members out of twelve, and ninety-five out of one hundred and twenty excisemen. Twenty-nine out of forty *Juges de Paix* are Protestants. In 1889, when the Bishop of Nimes died, the Government appointed a Protestant notary as trustee of his estate." The *Daily*

News correspondent, here quoted, adds: "The Catholics denounce this as intolerable oppression. But the truth is that the Protestants are, as a rule, highly educated, whilst the Catholic peasants are utterly illiterate."

This represents Protestantism at its best. We must not infer that there are many other counties, or even any, which could make at present so gratifying an exhibit as is afforded in the department of the Gard. In the great centers the numerical showing is small. Under Napoleon III, Protestantism was repressed, especially in the cities. Under the Republic, however, it has enjoyed, not only liberty, but a species of governmental encouragement. This new opportunity it is grandly using. There is great activity in Paris, and good results are attending it. The Reformed faith is not without its representatives in newspaper circles. It is a hopeful fact that the *Temps*, one of the most respectable of Paris journals, is of Protestant predilection, and it is equally gratifying to know that there is a religious journal in Paris whose name, *Le Huguenot*, sufficiently indicates its character, which is so prosperous that its circulation is maintained at 10,000 copies.

As an offset to this prosperity it ought to be mentioned that French Protestantism suffered a serious loss numerically by the war of 1870-71. In the two provinces taken by Germany the Protestant cause had something like 200,000 adherents. Most of these are gone, at least from the statistics of Protestantism in France.

The impartial observer, remembering what Germany did for the Huguenots in the time of their bloody trials, and that one of the finest churches in Berlin stands to this day as a monument of the asylum she afforded her persecuted brothers when France itself cast them out,—when one remembers this, it is impossible to begrudge to that nation the religious acquisition which the fortunes of battle have brought to her. But French Protestants feel differently, and one does not need to be long in their midst to see very clearly that patriotism, joined to a sense of denominational bereavement, makes the Franco-Prussian war a sad memory to them, and Germany a nation which does not in the least command their love.

We were interested to know the exact feeling of French Protestants upon the question of disestablishment, or, in other words, the withdrawal from all religions of the aid they now receive from the State. It has been remarked elsewhere that this could be done at any time by a simple refusal on the part of the Legislature to pass the budget for this purpose. That party in the Chamber known as the Left, and embracing the more advanced Radicals, has threatened that before long something of this kind will occur. Consequently it was a pertinent question with us, What are the probabilities of such a course, and how is it viewed by those Protestant Churches which are directly interested?

Our queries were addressed to Pastor Lorriaux, a scholarly and influential minister of the Reformed Church. Of course he could speak only for his own denomination; but when it is remembered that the Reformed Church embraces about five-sixths of all the Protestants in France, the views of this clergyman become singularly weighty. As to the prospect, Mr. Lorriaux was not apprehensive. Radicalism, he said, became more sober when it got into power. What men might threaten from irresponsible seats was often quite different from what they did as Cabinet ministers. It was distinctly recognized by Republicans of every shade that disestablishment would put a severe strain upon the existing form of government, and that it might even precipitate a civil war. To withdraw State aid from the priests would be to make them more bitter toward the Republic than they were even now, and what was more, it would touch the peasantry of the nation at the one point in which they were the most sensitive, their pockets.

"What does the average peasant care for liberty?" exclaimed our friend. "Such an appeal does not touch him. What he wants is a chance to support himself, and to enjoy without cost, as he may need them, the forms and ceremonies of the Church. Deprive him of these, or make the enjoyment of them burdensome, and you make an enemy of him. If the Republic should do this, he would become the enemy of the Republic, and would be ready for a change. He is not devout, but he is a great lover of Church ceremonials, and hence is in need of his priest. Besides which he is frugal—perhaps a little sordid—and wants everything as cheap as possible, including religion. It must not be forgotten either that the peasantry has the controlling electoral power. The revolutionary and publishing power is in the cities; the voting power is in the country."

These are the considerations, reported almost *verbatim*, which, in Mr. Lorriaux's judgment, make it extremely improbable that the existing status will be interfered with. "Nevertheless," said he, "disestablishment is a beautiful ideal, and it may finally be realized. It would leave us freer than we are, and would summon our Church to great sacrifices. So far it would be a gain. We Protestants are poor, as a rule, though there are some among us who are wealthy. We should sadly miss the little help we get from the State; but no doubt by a readjustment of our methods and a greater reliance upon God, we should survive, and should be able to carry forward our work. In the event of general disestablishment, Protestants would be greater sufferers relatively than Catholics, because they are fewer, poorer, and have less of social prestige. But we are not expecting such an event, nor are we taking active steps to bring it about. We recognize, however, that such a change is possible, and hence we are getting ready for it by strengthening our organization in various ways.

While not, perhaps, desiring disestablishment, we are not afraid of it, and we do not doubt that if it should come, God will bring safely through the storm—for storm it will be—both the Church and the nation."

By the same excellent authority we were enlightened upon another interesting subject; namely, the relative status within the Reformed Church of evangelicalism and rationalism. In substance what our kind informant said upon this topic was as follows: " When this Church was resurrected by Napoleon I, it was wholly rationalistic. Then came a great revival, and since that time rationalism has been steadily on the wane. At present its representatives in the ministry are from eighty to one hundred in a total of six hundred. Of two faculties of theology, both supported by the Government, that in Paris, which is rationalistic, has about fifty students; that at Montauban, which is evangelical, about eighty. Ministers of the rationalistic school are not aggressive. They do not preach against Christ; they simply refrain from preaching for him. All they ask now is to be let alone—a different attitude altogether from that formerly maintained. Many consistories have turned completely around from rationalism to sound evangelicalism. All the changes are of that kind; all the victories on that side. Rationalism has no life, and hence it makes no effort. From this point of view, the situation in French Protestantism is very gratifying, and the outlook extremely hopeful."

To confirm our own observations, and what we had learned by inquiry and reading, as to the opportunities presented to French Protestantism for an active campaign in behalf of the masses, an interview was sought with another leading minister, Jean Monnier. "We can go everywhere," said this noble descendant of the Huguenots, "and wherever we preach we have good results. Formerly we were restricted and hampered in our evangelizing efforts; now we are free. The large towns offer a very inviting field; but we think ourselves somewhat happy in the fact that, like the Apostle Paul, we find our most congenial sphere in the suburbs of such towns. Our missions in mining districts show a constant increase. One new Church has been built up into a membership of three hundred—all these having formerly been Roman Catholics. The workmen receive us gladly, and these constitute a fourth of the population. Among the middle and upper classes we make little headway, because these are strongly attached by tradition to Romanism. Occasionally, however, some of these come to us. For instance, M. Taine, the distinguished author, and heretofore a Catholic, has recently presented his daughter to Pastor Hollard to be received as a communicant in the Free Church. Amongst men of letters the conviction is spreading that without the religious life there is no hope for human society. We have tried philosophy, and its results are bad. Philosophy and science have raised new probems, and the young are looking for an explanation. They scarcely understand what they want; but they want something, and any one who can address them intelligently gains a hearing."

This is the situation as those see it who are in the thick of the fray. Possibly, however, the above estimate may mislead the reader upon one point, and that is, with reference to the drift from Catholicism to Protestantism. That there is such a drift is, happily, quite beyond question; nor can it be doubted that in some localities converts are made in considerable number. It is to be feared, however, that the gains to Protestantism from the ranks of disaffected Catholics are not large when viewed in the aggregate, and that relatively, at present, Protestant accessions bear but an indifferent proportion to Catholic losses. The real drift, as it seems to us, is toward atheism; though this, even if it be true, does not at all prove that French Protestantism is not doing what she can. It would rather seem to show that she has an enormous task cut out for her, and that in her noble effort to meet this crisis she deserves the sympathy and requires the help of her sister religionists throughout the wide world.

XX.

THE CONTINENTAL SUNDAY.

THE Sunday question is almost as live a topic in leading European nations as it has been for sometime in the United States. But over here the agitation and trend are decidedly favorable to a stricter observance of that day; whereas the clamor of large classes in our mixed American population is for change in the opposite direction. Viewing the day solely in its civil aspect as a day of rest, the difference between Europe and America seems to be that, on the eastern side of the Atlantic, there is an effort to realize the very conditions which, on the other side, are in danger of being wantonly given up. So marked are these opposite tendencies that, assuming their indefinite continuance, it is not impossible to imagine a time when Sunday will find, in European lands, its most zealous champions, and in America a state of things the precise counterpart of what has seemed to the American mind, as we have observed it in others, an example to be deprecated and shunned.

This new putting of the status of Sunday in Europe will awaken surprise in many quarters; and, to those who are ignorant of the latest developments over here, it will be so much of a novelty that they will hardly be able to credit it. The average American, we venture to believe, thinks of Sunday on the Continent as a hopeless cause; a day secularized quite beyond remedy; an institution with no friends to fight for it, and with scarcely enough vitality in it to provoke a discussion. We even suspect that this view is held in a mild form by not a few who have traveled in these lands. The Americans who visit Europe are here usually only as sight-seers. With rare exceptions they scarcely ever inquire about institutions and laws; they seldom penetrate beneath the surface of things; and as for the Sabbath, it is notorious that very many American tourists seem so fully convinced that nobody over here cares for it that they cease very soon to show any regard for it themselves. Spite of all, however, there is such a thing as Sabbath observance even on the Continent of Europe; and it will interest and gratify the better class of our readers—especially the working-class—to be assured, by one who has investigated the subject, that in France and Germany the day is so much better regarded than it used to be as to afford reasonable hope that it will become eventually, if not a strictly religious holiday, at least a day on which all business and labor will be suspended.

In Berlin, at the time we write, the Sunday question is the question of the hour. One thing which shows this, is the zeal of those who stand up for the old order of things. In his lecture at the university, a few days ago, Professor Von Treitschke, the great Prussian historian, digressed from his theme to say, with pronounced emphasis: "We don't want the American Sunday— we are satisfied with the German Sunday." Undoubtedly many of the people are satisfied, but some are not; and this is notably the case with those to whom the German Sunday has been heretofore a day of toil, with nothing to distinguish it from other days. Not only are the latter dissatisfied with the German Sunday, but their complaints have found potential expression, and have been incorporated within recent months into a law of the Reichstag.

This law makes long strides toward the prohibition in Germany of all Sunday labor. It affects factories, workshops, offices, stores, and almost every other place either of manufacture or merchandise. In many departments Sunday labor must be stopped altogether, and it must be brought down to the minimum in every department. Such is the new law in Germany. Its effects in Berlin are very marked. The shops now can be kept open not more than five hours on Sundays. These hours must never infringe upon Church hours; and, what is more, when the shops are closed they must be shut up tightly. Even the windows must be closed— an improvised curtain being required where shutters are lacking; and one of the best evidences that Germany is in earnest in this reform is that the police, so far, have fearlessly done their duty.

It is quite true that these conditions are not ideal. The reform, indeed, is a very partial one; and when it is remembered that these new regulations do not affect in the least the ever-privileged drinking-saloon, the situation becomes more unsatisfactory still. But the new *régime* is a decided improvement on the one it supplants; and however far this advance may fall short of what is needed, it certainly indicates progress. One has to remember, however, that it is not a religious movement either in its origin or intent. It is quite in harmony with religion in so far as it restricts from Sunday labor and suspends business on that day; but the enactment of this law, we have been assured, was not in the least due to any action on the part of the Churches, nor to any desire to keep Sunday as a holy day. It is strictly a working-class reform. It originated in the demand of this class for a day of rest from secular toil; and, as all are agreed, it was taken up by the Government largely as a matter of policy, because it was pushed so urgently by that growing party in German politics known as the Social Democrats.

In regard to France, if one may judge of the nation generally by what is obvious in Paris, the improvement here is little less marked than in the dominions of the Kaiser. With this difference, however, that the changes in the former of these countries are due solely to the force of sentiment, without, as yet, any advanced action of the Legislature on the subject. But if the recent years have witnessed no change in the French law, they have at least brought forth one very tangible thing, and that is a Sunday Observance Society. Its full French title is, "La Ligue Populaire pour le Repos du Dimanche en France." The first president of this League was M. Jules Simon, and the gentleman now filling that office is M. Leon Say. Both are members of the French Academy, and besides being eminent in literature, they are distinguished in political life. Jules Simon is a senator, and one of the finest orators in France, while Leon Say is an eloquent and influential deputy. Neither of these gentlemen is a pronounced Christian, though the last named is nominally a Protestant.

This Society, however, is in no sense a religious body, nor does it profess to seek religious ends. Senator Jules Simon said of it, some time ago: "We desire that our workmen may have a day's rest once a week, and Sunday is naturally the day we have chosen. But our undertaking is a difficult one, because it runs counter to numerous customs and interests. Two years ago our Society numbered twenty persons; to-day we count over 2,500 members, made up of Republicans, Monarchists, Catholics and Protestants, bishops and Freethinkers. We have already achieved some practical results. In the post-office we have got the hours shortened on Sunday, and we are now laboring with the railroad companies."

These words sufficiently disclose both the objects of this Society and the rapid growth it has had. But as an index of what the recent past has witnessed in Paris in the way of Sunday reform, they are too modest altogether. Some of the signs of improvement the visitor to this city can see with his own eyes; but to get the broadest and truest view, one must converse on this subject with intelligent and progressive Frenchmen. Twenty years have wrought changes for the better which are truly marvelous. No statistics are available, but the best judges hold that within that period the number of workmen following their ordinary occupations on Sunday has been reduced by more than one-half. In railway circles the chief reform is in the Sunday delivery of goods. Formerly this was carried on all day long; now it is only done in the morning. As to the retail stores, the common notion is that they are all open, with rare exceptions, at all hours on Sunday, and that the heaviest trade is done on that day. This, however, is a scandalous fallacy. Such a notion may have had only too good a foundation in times gone by, but the Parisian Sunday of to-day is almost as different in this matter from what it was formerly as Paris itself is from the aspect it presented prior to the Third Napoleon's time.

At present many of the stores do not open at all on Sunday, and many of those which do open are closed again after a few hours. This is especially noticeable in those quarters where the best class of trade is done. In poorer quarters, as a matter of course, the improvement is less marked; and it need hardly be said that cafés, and places of that kind, are no more affected by this change of sentiment in Paris than they are by the wholesome but inadequate laws which regulate the Sunday traffic of Berlin. As to the post-office, it is quite true that a number of deliveries have been dispensed with; but the postman still waits upon you several times in the forenoon, and experience has shown us that on Sundays—as on other days—you can be troubled with letters very late at night. It is gratifying to note, however, that, excepting in those lines in which the letting out of the fires would involve considerable loss, manufacturing is very generally at a standstill during the hours of Sunday; and the same may be said also, with even less allowance for exceptions, of the great wholesale trade of this city.

A Parisian gentleman, who is very prominent in literary and philanthropic circles, pointed us with pride to the Sunday aspect worn at the present day by the Rue Aboukir. This is the very heart of the wholesale quarter. "Forty years ago," he observed, "my father-in-law, a wholesale woolen dealer, moved into that street from the north of France. With him he brought his custom of resting from business on Sunday. To the amazement and disgust of those about him he persevered in this custom. He would neither be laughed out of it by ridicule, nor frightened out of it by predictions which foretold his ultimate bankruptcy. Finally, seeing that he continued to prosper, others followed his example; and the course of some years witnessed the closing on Sundays of every wholesale house in that neighborhood, which is now as much characterized by an air of Sabbath repose as the wholesale parts of London itself."

Such an instance as this, besides showing how much good may be done by a worthy example, shows at a flash also how, in recent years, this city of Paris, which very many have thought hopelessly wedded to Sabbath traffic, has been gradually emancipating itself and taking on better habits. She is still very far, of course—just as is Berlin—from approximating to either English or American ideals; but one has only to look about him, with eyes and ears open, and to inquire with unbiased mind, in well-informed and well-disposed circles, to discover in both these cities a decided improvement, and fully to convince himself that both cities are traveling in the right direction.

In regard to amusements and recreations, there is little or no change; and what makes the prospect in this direction particularly gloomy, from the point of view occupied by Christian Americans, is that, all over the Continent, there seems to be an utter lack of conscience on this subject. With the exception of a small evangelical contingent, which is almost wholly confined to missionary Churches, the Protestants of France and Germany seem to be no more scrupulous in these matters than their Roman Catholic neighbors. To give an example, we were in conversation recently with one of the most devout and learned of the pastors of the Reformed Church of France, and in answer to our question as to what would be expected from his members in the way of Sunday observance, his reply was that it would not be in the least improper, after attendance at Church in the morning, to occupy the afternoon in a visit to the Louvre or in a ramble through one of the parks; and as to his young men, he did not feel at all warranted in cautioning them against the little games of lawn-tennis they played on Sunday, because they were constantly offered in Paris so many diversions that were immoral.

This same gentleman, however, was unstinted in his commendation of the good work going forward under the patronage of men like Jules Simon and Leon Say; and it really appears as though, upon the cardinal point of reducing to a minimum all Sunday labor, the best minds of France, whether evangelical or atheistic, Catholic or Protestant, are in unanimous and hearty agreement.

XXI.

FRENCH HOLIDAY-MAKING.

THE French character runs to extremes. It would be hard to find a people who follow more industriously their daily avocations, and, on the other hand, it would be difficult to match them in the wild abandonment with which their national holidays are observed. It is noteworthy, too, that most of their holidays are "holy days," which had their origin, and still find their center of interest, in the Catholic Church. In all her efforts to throw off the trammels of Romanism—some of which have been carried very far—this nation has shown no eagerness up to the present to ignore the grand fêtes of that Church, and while high and low shall continue to be as fond as they now are of occasions for gayety and display, a crusade of this kind is hardly to be expected.

Among the lesser holidays are the Ascension in May, the Assumption in August, and All Saints' Day on November 1st. The Church, of course, has numerous other gala-days of greater or less importance; but these three are amongst the days which the nation has fixed upon, and still sacredly observes, as occasions when the banks are closed, and when the populace generally has governmental sanction for turning out to enjoy itself. The brightest of these three days is that devoted to the blessed Virgin. The Churches on that day are a mass of floral whiteness. It is also customary on this day to present white flowers to those girls whose fond mammas had them christened *Marie*, and as about every other French damsel is the happy possessor of that name, it is a great day for French florists and correspondingly a time of depletion for French purses. All Saints is a sadder time, because it immediately precedes All Souls' Day, when the French people pour *en masse* into their cemeteries to lay floral emblems on the resting-places of their dead. In fact, All Saints' Day itself is largely employed in pathetic services of this kind, and if one would form a true idea of the extreme lengths to which the French people go in the observance of this custom, he must visit the graveyards, as we did, and witness this deeply impressive spectacle for himself. To see the profusion of flowers the day after All Souls, is something one can never forget, and, really, what one sees in our own cemeteries after Decoration-day is hardly a circumstance to the way in which the French attend to such matters.

Christmas is another national holiday; but the nation, for some reason, has not made of this fête anything like the great occasion which it is either in Germany or in countries where English is spoken. The Churches observe it, as a matter of course, with the pomp usual in Roman Catholic strongholds, and with some extras as a tribute to the French love for realistic art. The midnight mass is a great function, and the Government, by the way, seems so bent upon making it exclusively a French affair, that the few foreign Churches in Paris which observe it, have to pay an exorbitant tax for the privilege. Another striking feature is the reproduction before one of the altars of the familiar Birth-scene. Nearly all the Churches furnish a Christmas attraction of this kind; but the Church which generally excels in spectacular effects is St. Roche's, in the Rue St. Honoré. Joseph and Mary are there, life-size, and modeled after the best portraits. So are the patient cows, and the beast of burden which had brought the Holy Mother to Bethlehem. To help the illusion, there is also a manger with plenty of straw scattered about, but the central and most interesting figure is a wax model of the Holy Child.

Until very recently the French have taken no stock in Santa Claus, in Christmas-trees, in what the English call "Christmas boxes," or even in our own American craze for the pretty cards fashionable at that season. But the country, in these latter days, is being favored or afflicted—which the reader pleases—by an invasion of ideas and customs from the other side of the Channel. In other words, the *bon ton* of French society is becoming "English, you know." To dress after the English fashion is quite the swell thing now with men in the upper circles. Not only have English trousers come over, but the fashion of turning them up at the boots has captured the

French mind; and among the numerous other habits which the French are contracting from the English, is that of observing Christmas. This, however, is only in Paris and the larger towns in the Provinces. Elsewhere the day is scarcely marked at all by the features which signalize it in the United States. In fact, in every respect, excepting as a bank-holiday and a feast of the Church, it seems to be passed by unnoticed in the wild anticipation with which everybody just then is looking forward to the New-Year.

To show at a flash how much is made of New-Year's day in France we mention a single circumstance. At the time we write, the comment of some of the papers upon the new ministry which has come into power, is this: That about the only thing which can save it from summary overthrow is the near approach of that French holiday which is sacredly set apart by all classes to the cultivation and expression of good fellowship. In its social aspects this day is everything to the Frenchman that Christmas and Thanksgiving are to the American, and even more. The grand Parisian shops, instead of putting out a Christmas display, announce in blazing characters their "*exposition des étrennes*," which means a display of the most costly and tempting New-Year's gifts. Costly is the true word for some of these gifts; for how else can you speak of elaborate boxes of bonbons at from fifty to a hundred francs each, or of ravishing dolls, which, if you bought them, would make as big a vacuum in your pocket-book as an ordinary bridal trousseau?

In Paris the coming of this great holiday is indicated by a transformation on the Great Boulevards. From the Madeleine to the end of Boulevard des Italiens the broad sidewalks are skirted with booths—*Barraques du jour de l'an,* is their French cognomen. In these all sorts of toys and fancy goods are for sale; fortunately, too, at prices which appeal to the masses. Every year some new toy comes out, and so great is Paris on following the fashion, that this novelty, be it pretty or ugly, useful or superfluous, becomes the rage of the hour, and, in consequence, the final possession of every child in the town. This, moreover, is another season when florists do a big business; for wherever a gentleman may have taken dinner occasionally, he must send at New-Year's some token of grateful remembrance. Otherwise, hospitality is likely to be withdrawn; and these tributes, as a rule, take the form of an exquisite bouquet, or perhaps, if there is a *mademoiselle* in the house, the gift is a dainty assortment of sweets.

These, however, are trifling matters, which, in the sum total of New-Year's customs, make scarcely any figure. In addition to the universal exchange of presents between friends, there are your servants and dependents to be looked after. None of these can be slighted, if you value either your standing or your peace of mind, and to some the gifts must be of substantial value. Such a wishing of *Bonne Année* as there is all around at this season would do one's heart good, were it not for the knowledge you have that almost every one who wishes you a good year, wishes also to be remembered by a good present. Everybody who has served you, or who has been ready to serve you, wishes you well—the butcher's boy, the baker's boy, the street-sweeper, the milkman, the lamplighter, and, in fact, all sorts and conditions of people, some of whom you never have seen before, and will not see again, perhaps, for another twelvemonth. In fact, it is just as it is at Christmas time in America, only a hundred times more so.

Here, as in England, the postman comes in for one of your largest bounties, and we only wish that the French postal system rendered its representatives as worthy as the English of what is annually meted out to them at this season. But if the system is not a very deserving one, the letter-carriers themselves are worthy enough; and when one thinks of the enormous amount of extra work the New-Year entails, one can hardly begrudge the five or ten francs they expect in the form of a New-Year's largess. Which reminds us of another French custom—that of exchanging *cartes de visite* at this season. Everybody does it with everybody he knows. The ordinary calling-card is used, and the custom is so extensive that these missives are received at the post-offices in separate boxes. To handle them in connection with the other mails would interfere seriously with business. As it is, however, they are distributed and dispatched at the convenience of the officials, and it sometimes happens that the enormous pile is not entirely cleared until the New-Year is three or four weeks old.

A distinctively French functionary is the *concierge*. He is literally ubiquitous in the cities and towns. You pass his room—or hers, as the case may be—every time you enter or leave your apartment. However late you may come in at night, the *concierge*, by some attachment near his bed, unfastens the door for you. He receives your letters, stands in with the servants for every bit of gossip about your affairs, and collects regularly the rent you may pay. For these and various other purposes he is hired by the landlord, but much of his keep is drawn from the tenants in the shape of tips and fees. You will never go amiss in making a present to this functionary, and what is appropriate and wise at any time, becomes at New-Year's your solemn and never-to-be-forgotten duty. An expensive one, too; for if you are living in fairly good style, it will cost you from a hundred to two hundred francs.

It is pleasant to know that the New-Year is a time when the poor are specially remembered. As this season approaches, the people are universally appealed to, through the Bureau of Public Assistance, for a special contribution of money, and few are the families who do not respond. This Bureau operates through local societies which exist in every municipality, and a part of that which is collected just before the New-Year begins is given out on New-Year's day as a special bounty to those in need; the rest being kept as a fund for the more systematic relief of poverty all the year through. In addition to this, New-Year's day is marked by a free outflow of private benevolence. Many will be the calls at your door, and, if you are in a typical French family, you will find that hardly any caller is sent empty away.

In France, too, our own American custom of making New-Year's calls is in vogue; but this function, which is falling into disuse with us, is still, as it always has been, the life and soul of the New-Year to a Frenchman. Every public official is duly visited by every subordinate, and as for the President of the Republic, his palace in the Champs Elysées is besieged all day long. The entire diplomatic corps wait upon him on New-Year's day, and an interminable string of other carriage-folk. But not the commoners, for the French President is surrounded by more fuss and feathers than the occupant of the White House, and he draws a strict line socially even at New-Year's.

Turkey and truffles is the great dish for a stylish New-Year's dinner. The truffles are steeped in Madeira wine, and, after being sliced, are inserted between the skin and the meat of this luscious fowl. This, however, is a luxury which only the rich can enjoy in France. Among the peasants the New-Year is pig-killing time, and a little pork is the peasant's special relish for the New Year's dinner. But whatever the fare on the table, there is always good feeling in the heart, and always plenty of good company at the fireside. Not only must the members of the household sit down together on New-Year's day, but, if possible, the relatives must be gathered in, even to the most distant cousin; and one of the very happiest of all the New-Year's customs is that which seizes upon the day as a suitable time for healing the breaches of friendship, and for smoking the pipe of peace over quarrels which have divided families.

XXII.

POVERTY AND WEALTH.

FROM some points of view the material condition of the French nation is gratifying in the extreme. She is often described as the richest nation in Europe, not excepting her near neighbor and only European rival—Great Britain. It is very certain that property, both real and personal, is more evenly distributed in France than in England, even if it does not aggregate as much. To be told that of the ten millions of houses in this country one-half are occupied exclusively by their respective owners, affords us a glimpse of French prosperity which seems almost too good to be true. Another discovery equally astonishing is to find the landed proprietors estimated at eight millions or more, and to be assured from statistics that one-half of all the soil devoted to agriculture is cultivated by the individuals to whom it belongs. In these respects Great Britain is thrown completely into the shade; and it becomes unquestionable that, in so far as the general diffusion of wealth can contribute to national greatness, France is without a peer among all the great powers of the world.

In the inquiries we have made regarding the solvency of the French Government, we have been met everywhere by the remark that an infallible proof of this is afforded at every fresh appeal for a national loan. The amount required is subscribed for in such cases with an alacrity which ought, they say, to convince the most skeptical; and it is the judgment of patriotic Frenchmen that there has been no time in recent years when the Government could not have obtained, without the least trouble, ten times as much as it has asked for. This is decidedly assuring, if it is true; for there can be no doubt that there is plenty of money in the country, and if the numerous holders of it are as ready as we are led to believe to trust the Government with it, there ought to be no trouble in providing either for current expenses, or for such enormous drafts as another great war would involve.

Upon this point a very interesting writer, M. Betham-Edwards, has said:

"We can understand how the German war indemnity of two hundred million sterling was paid when we see the country folks on dividend-day. I happened to be at a friend's house at Dijon upon one of these occasions, and he asked if I would like to accompany him to the *Recette Générale*, or local branch of the State bank. Before starting with his own dividends and those of his family, he went up-stairs to the kitchen, and fetched the servants. True enough, all were fund-holders—one to a considerable extent. Arrived at the office, it was a sight to see the motley crowd flocking in with their coupons—important functionaries, fashionable ladies, laundresses and charwomen in neat caps, laborers and artisans in blue blouses—all contentedly awaiting their turn. Nothing ever brought more forcibly home to my mind the thrift of the French nation—the forethought which brings about a very real and enviable equality."

The most astounding thing we have seen in France is the Eiffel Tower. It looks so big and high, when you stand near to it, as almost to make one shudder at the sense of its unearthliness. We refer to this here because it is this mammoth product of the genius of French engineering which is seized upon by French statisticians as the one object best fitted to image before our minds the mammoth dimensions of the French faculty for saving money. The Eiffel Tower, we are told by M. de Foville, weighs from seven to eight million kilogrammes—the kilogramme being two pounds and 3.62 ounces. Yet if this tower were reconstructed of solid silver, it would represent the existing deposits of the French people in the national savings banks, says this authority, only after two additional stories had been added to it—the sum total of these deposits amounting to two milliards of francs. Then follows another unearthly comparison. A milliard, says M. de Foville, is not a figure easily grasped by the mind, for not a milliard of minutes have yet elapsed since the Christian era.

The Postal Savings Bank was instituted in 1882. It has now about seven thousand branch offices, and its clients are so numerous that they represent nearly an eighteenth part of the population of France and Algiers combined. The interest paid is only three per cent, and that so many should be content to receive this is an indication either that other opportunities for investment are not numerous, or that they have not the hold the Government has on the popular confidence. Most of the deposits, as a matter of course, are small. One-half of the two million of investors have to their credit a less amount than $20. The latest statistics accessible as we write show that within the year new accounts had been opened to the number of 348,695; and, as an indication of the extent to which the national thrift is shared in by the fair sex, it is worth noting that 150,787 of these were opened by women.

That these evidences of national prosperity are not misleading is strikingly shown in a recent report of Mr. Horace G. Knowles, United States consul at Bordeaux. This report devotes special attention to the growth of French prosperity during the past twenty years. Since the fall of the Second Empire, for example, the production of coal in France has increased 90 per cent, and its consumption by 71 per cent. The tonnage of the goods transported by railway has increased 87 per per cent; the number of travelers by rail has doubled; postal business has augmented by 140 per cent; the cash reserve in the Bank of France has doubled; between 1869 and 1891 the funds in the French savings banks increased fourfold; people throughout the country are in easier circumstances; and, as this report says, "if the burden now laid upon the taxpayer is heavier than formerly, he has, to say the least, greater resources at his disposal. Under no *régime* has wealth in France developed with such rapid strides as under the present system of government."

All this is very true, but unfortunately the prosperity of the nation under the Republic has a reverse side to it; for during this time those in power have been piling up an enormous debt, which amounts now to not far from six billions of dollars. The national debt of France is considerably more than twice what it was when the Empire went down. It is quite true that the chief cause of this vast increase was the disastrous war into which the nation was precipitated by Napoleon III. But that is long ago, and, unfortunately, the debt of France still grows. What is more, and worse, the revenues at present seem quite inadequate to the financial drain it imposes. Fancy the difficulty of meeting an annual call for something like two hundred and sixty million dollars in interest and annuities!

If a national debt is—as some one has called it—a national blessing, France ought to be very happy and very proud. No other nation is blessed as she in this respect, or anything like it. Russia comes next, with a debt of about three and a half billion dollars. But Russia, with a national debt only seven-twelfths as large, has a population back of it which is more than twice that of France. The English debt is about the same as that of Russia; while the Prussian Government has only to carry, as against the six billions of France, a solitary one billion of dollars—indeed, a little less than that. England and Germany, moreover, have their national indebtedness so well in hand, and are so well provided with permanent revenues for taking care of it, that they could carry the incubus without strain for an indefinite period. But the French system is a system of expedients and makeshifts. Those who have carefully observed it, say that it is the "hand-to-mouth principle," and that the vital difference between Germany and France is, that Germany could go on as she is now doing and see her national debt finally extinguished, whereas France can only look forward under existing conditions—the question of war left out of the account altogether—to increasing embarrassment, issuing finally in a great crisis.

This is what the wiseacres of finance tell us, and of course they have the figures with which to back up their statements. But, for our part, we do not doubt that a nation which has so much wealth in it, and which is pre-eminent amongst European powers for the large number of its citizens who have money in the bank, will not only continue to raise whatever may be needed for emergencies, but will get her national finances into such condition before long that everything will move smoothly, and the obvious trend of all be toward increasing strength, rather than possible catastrophe. As an evidence of French shrewdness on a large scale, we have heard it said that the nation in twenty years has made enough money out of its monopoly of matches to pay the German war indemnity. This, of course, is an exaggeration. But out of the two monopolies of matches and tobacco she has made far more than enough for that purpose; and it is our judgment that a nation which can do this will not end in smoke very soon, and will prove more than a match finally for even the stupendous national debt she has incurred.

Every country, even the most prosperous, has its problem of poverty to deal with; and France, in spite of her unparalleled diffusion of wealth, is no exception to this rule. France, however, is far from having the great mass of poor that England has. This is due chiefly, no doubt, to those economic conditions which make it possible for so many of her toiling citizens to acquire land, and to live in their own houses; but the superior thrift of the French has something to do with it. And still another reason why dependence is less common in France than in England is, that it has been less encouraged there. The English system provides that every family not able to live by its own efforts may obtain, by legal right, a subsistence from the parish, and, at the last extremity, find a shelter, such as it is, in some poor-house. Poverty is a recognized institution there, and the poor-rate an ever-present terror to all householders.

In France it is different. There is no poor-rate, and the only persons who have a legal right to Government support are lunatics and orphans. These it cares for partly in a few buildings of its own, and in still larger part by paying for their support elsewhere. Hospitals for the sick and asylums for the infirm are either private or Communal enterprises. The Government, however, contributes to their expenses and exercises supervision over them. This matter is devolved by law upon the Ministry of the Interior, and is attended to by a department called the Assistance Publique. Its funds are derived from a variety of sources, and it operates in every Commune. The amount annually expended for the indoor and outdoor relief of the sick, aged, and infirm—including orphans and lunatics—is about thirty million dollars. The Government furnishes a part of this fund, and it often benefits by bequests. Once a year, too, the citizens generally are appealed to in behalf of it; though perhaps the most interesting fact of all is that the Assistance Publique of France draws a considerable portion of its revenues from a tax on the gross receipts at all theatrical performances, and from the betting which forms so large a feature at the numerous horse-races.

XXIII.

THE WAR-CLOUD.

AMERICANS who are so exceptional as not to have visited Europe think it strange that European correspondents give such prominence as they do to military affairs, and wonder why it is that these worthy gentlemen treat the American public as regularly as the spring opens to sensational predictions of an impending European war. The time was when we were perplexed upon these points ourself, but we think now that we fully understand the matter. A little, of course, must be allowed for newspaper "enterprise"— and you can spell the word with a big "E," if you like, and leave room in it for a considerable exercise of the imaginative faculties; but this is only a partial explanation. To do full justice, the question of environment must be taken into account. One breathes in Europe a military atmosphere. The armaments of these nations are the biggest things about them. The question of war or peace is nearly always the question of the hour, and national happiness waits continually upon the answer. From this point of view the difference between the United States and France is the difference between a nation with a standing army of twenty-five thousand, and another nation, not much more than half as populous, which has a standing army of about a million and a quarter, with men enough in its reserve forces to swell the number to over four millions. To put the contrast in another light, there are twice as many soldiers in Paris alone as you could drum up to-day within the far-reaching limits of our entire Nation.

After residing here for a time one gets an inkling of the significance of these figures, and of the awful possibilities they open up as regards the future. The dilemma which confronts you is this—either that the French people are a nation of fools, bent on bankrupting themselves without any good reason; or, that they are a nation over whose heads a tremendous war-cloud impends, which may break at any time with such destructive fury as to threaten their very existence. Perhaps they are fools anyway. Perhaps all these Continental peoples are fools. This doesn't seem at all improbable when you remember that every century the battle-fields of Europe absorb the life-blood of eighteen or twenty millions of her flowering manhood, and that Germany, after her great victory over France, spent the billion dollars of indemnity she exacted in strengthening her defenses, and has since laid out on her army more than three billions of dollars taken out of the pockets of her own people. But here again the question of environment comes in; for if one nation in Europe does it, they must all do it. So they say over here, at least; and, after studying the situation at close range, it is difficult to see how either France or Germany could do, in the circumstances in which they are placed, any differently from what they are doing.

On the surface of things it would appear as though all these elaborate preparations for war were, after all, the best possible guarantee of continued peace. Germany, it is quite certain, has been less inclined to precipitate a conflict with France since 1889, when the latter, by a sweeping war measure, made army service practically universal. It is certain, too, that when the new army measures have been completed on the other side of the Rhine, France will be less inclined than before to renew hostilities against Germany. And still another safeguard arising from the extension of military conscriptions is, that the further they extend, the more they involve the nation as a whole, and the more, in consequence, do they make the question of war or peace one in which the whole nation is personally interested. In France, where the Government is strictly representative, this is particularly the case. This nation is no longer a plaything for kings. It is not within the power of an emperor or a president to let loose her dogs of war. If war shall come, it will be because the people shall so decree; and since the people are the army—every family contributing its contingent—it would seem to be only a plausible supposition that they will move cautiously, and, before drawing the sword, pause a little time to count the cost, and see if such a dire extremity may not by some means be averted.

This is how one could wish it to be, and how the surface facts would warrant us in expecting that it will be; but there is, unfortunately, another side to this fair picture. It is quite true as regards France that the initiative of war rests with the great body of the people; but it is equally true that the people of this nation are resting at present under the humiliation of a crushing defeat, and that, with scarcely an exception, they cherish feelings of bitterness, perhaps even of vindictiveness, toward the nation which chastised them. In moving amongst the French people it becomes painfully evident to even the most casual observer that the present peace is looked upon merely as a truce between two engagements—that the battle for final supremacy has yet to come, and that the French people, while they may fear to hasten that final duel, will not seek to avoid it, and will consider their situation permanently tranquil only when it has been fought and won.

The French are exceedingly sensitive. Proud of their history as a nation of fighters, and with a passion for military glory such as no other of the great powers of Europe has shown, it is hardly to be expected that they would accept German domination as a permanency without at least one effort to rid themselves of it; and, of course, their partial dismemberment, by the annexation to Germany of Alsace and Lorraine, makes this additionally unlikely. That Russian diplomat who, after the treaty of Frankfort, congratulated the Iron Chancellor upon having annexed an open wound, did not miss the mark very far. The annexed provinces are wounds indeed, and they have any amount of proud-flesh in them. An index of French feeling on the subject is afforded constantly in the Place de la Concorde, where the Statue of Strasburg is almost always decorated with emblems of national mourning; and, what is still more suggestive, you can see in some of the shop-windows a photograph of this statue, with the inscription beneath it: "Taken by the Germans, 1870. Retaken by the French, 189–."

These are only straws, to be sure, but they show plainly enough in what direction the popular feeling is set. Recently, too, was French sensitiveness on this subject put to a rather severe strain, the offending party being, unfortunately, the German chancellor, Count Von Caprivi. His great army-bill speech was, in one view, decidedly flattering to French vanity. It is quite certain that ordinarily the French would not object to hearing their capital spoken of as "a fortified city such as the world has never known before," or to be reminded that their forts are "equipped with all the strength of modern science," and that they have "army corps which are very different from those of 1870." Such sayings would make sweet music in French ears, assuming their source to be agreeable and their motive above suspicion. But when Caprivi says these things for the purpose of converting the Germans to his own view of their enhanced military requirements, and when in saying them he takes the German army across the western frontier, and in thought plants it once more before the walls of Paris, the case is so altered that compliments become almost as stinging as bullets would be.

French feeling was deeply touched by this speech. "Peace was the pretext," said a member of the Cabinet, commenting upon it, "but war was the subject. M. de Caprivi not only says publicly that war is possible, but he even dwells lovingly upon the spectacle which the German army would witness were it to enter French territory. I am well aware that M. de Caprivi is a general, and that this sort of talk must seem quite natural to him; but he is also an imperial chancellor, upon whom depend the diplomatic relations between his country and other powers, and he assuredly ought not to speak in that style. Under the circumstances we could almost wish that he would be less pacific, if he would be more respectful of parliamentary usage, in his language."

A very palpable proof that the bent of France is in the direction of war is seen every day in the effusive sentimentality of the nation toward Russia. The Russian royalties are the biggest lions the French capital ever entertains, and the Russian flag is seen so often in loving company with the tricolor that you could almost imagine the two flags were one, with but a single thought. That the Russian Bear and the Republican Lamb should be on terms of such gushing familiarity is a singular spectacle, and there can be only one explanation of it.

Another warlike symptom is the great popularity of the army, and the comparative cheerfulness with which the nation, at enormous expense, has resolved itself within a few years into a universal military camp. Germany submits to new exactions with reluctance. She chafes and kicks under a military system which would have to be far more severe than it is to tax the nation either in pocket or person as the French are taxed. In Germany, at present, the contribution per head for national defense is only about two-thirds as much as the people of France are paying, and general taxation there does not amount per head to even one-half what it is here. The fact is, no people in Europe are taxed as the French are, and the reason they submit with so good a grace is undoubtedly because their feelings are aroused. They have a great loss to retrieve and a wounded spirit to avenge; and the way in which at present they pay out their money in taxes is only too palpable an earnest of how, when the need arises, they will pour out their blood in this cause.

Paradoxical as it may seem, the least warlike of all the things one sees in France is the physique of the average French soldier. You meet plenty of military men on the streets of Paris, but one could hardly be afraid of them. They look decidedly pretty, but not at all formidable. There are many exceptions, of course; but the general run of these "soldier boys" are boyish-looking in the extreme, with short, slender frames, and with hardly enough masculinity in them—so it would seem—to bristle out into even a vigorous-looking military mustache. As regards officers, the specimens you see on the streets of Berlin are a race of giants in comparison with those who trip daintily along the boulevards of Paris. Man to man, the French would surely have no chance. But the coming war will be one of strategy and science, not one of brute force. The fighting will be done by machines and brains, and if the French are superior to the Germans in their possession of these requisites, they may come off victorious, spite of their disproportionate stature—especially if their army shall retain until that time its present numerical supremacy.

This question of peace or war is linked in France to another grave question. If those in power should discern the time when a blow could be struck with the certainty of success, and should then proceed to strike it, winning back the two lamented provinces and treating the Germans as the French themselves were treated a couple of decades ago, it would not be asked again—certainly not for many years—whether the Republic had come to stay. Such a victory would do more to establish the existing form of government than could be done in twenty years of peace, even if those years were unvaryingly prosperous. The test of war has yet to come to this regenerated nation, and until that has been reached and safely passed, the man who should say that the Republic is necessarily permanent would either be very rash or very ignorant. The French people become desperate under defeat; and in the event of a repetition of the disasters of '71, it is difficult to believe, after all we know of the French temperament and of French history, that the Republican Government, as it exists to-day, would fare any better than the Government of Napoleon did. But as to this, if we live long enough, we shall see for ourselves.

XXIV.

CONTRASTS AND CONCLUSIONS.

HARDLY anything in French life has impressed us more forcibly than the many striking contrasts it presents. We have always known that humanity was a bundle of contradictions, but our studies of French humanity have strengthened this conviction a hundredfold. Assuming variety to be the spice of life, the French, it must be admitted, are a highly-seasoned people; and it is perhaps not too much to say that, from this point of view, they are the most interesting nationality in Europe. Just as French artists excel in the niceties of light and shadow, so it is in the daily life of the French people as a whole. The lights are very distinct, and these, unfortunately, are no more pleasing than the shadows are repulsive and ominous. To begin with material things, it is in France that you find frugality more fully exemplified than in other modern nations; and here also do you find the love of dress and the craving for table indulgences carried to such an unparalleled extent that it vitiates the morals, and, as French writers themselves do not hesitate to declare, acts as a restraint on the natural growth one ought to find in population. As to money, people in France affect to scorn it as a solace for blighted affections and wounded honor. In affairs of this kind the revolver is preferred to breach of promise suits, and cold steel to damages for libel. None the less, however, French shopkeepers, to make all they can out of a rapacious public, do nearly all their trade on the bargain and barter principle, and the people generally are such evident lovers of filthy lucre that even marriage is invested with a distinctly mercantile aspect; while, in further proof, one needs only to recall the Panama revelations, which indicate at once the prevalence of the gambling instinct among the poor of France, and the fascination exercised by the gains of gambling over many who are better off in the world.

To skip from material to religious tendencies, it may surely be said of the chief city of France that it is a city of churches; and yet it is just as true, and far more customary, to speak of it as a city of pleasure, not to mention the still more unsavory names which are sometimes given to it. Our Lady of Lourdes, with the superstitions which cluster about her shrine, is no more really a French character than the lady of fashion, with crowds of weak-headed masculinity draggling in her train. How much of open and incipient unbelief there is in France is but too apparent on every hand; yet side by side with this, there is so much faith in the supernatural that religious retreats are still numerous, and men and women to be found everywhere so absorbed in the thought of a future life that present hardship is a joy to them. As an English writer has said, "France is the country of the woman of the world, *la mondaine*, and of the Carmelite nun—the one living in the utmost luxury, the other in the hardest austerity— and a gleam of hope or a cloud of disappointment in the life of a young lady may determine for her which of the two she is to be."

Still looking for contrasts, we turn now to the social aspects of French life, beginning, as we ought, with the home. Everybody knows how strong and tender are family ties in this country, and the most casual observer must also see what a painful lack there is of genuine home-life. It is the country of which we are told that its young men have a remarkable fondness for their mothers; and, by a strange paradox, it is also the country of which we know that the place of predilection for the great mass of its young life is not the home-circle, but the café. In regard to girlhood, the home and school surveillance is so strict as to savor somewhat of the Oriental system, while, as regards a large section of its female society beyond the pale of home-life, the rules of conduct are so lax as to suggest Orientalism of quite another kind. It is only within recent years that France has re-enacted a divorce law. How she managed to get along without one was always a mystery to us, and when we now learn that the number of divorces in 1891 was 5,752, with the annual output steadily increasing, our surprise is deepened. Against

England's annual showing of less than 300 divorces, these figures exhibit France in a dreadful light; and she is evidently worse behaved in this matter, though not very much so, than her sister Republic over the sea.

Looking now at social life in its broader phases, the contrasts which meet us are no less striking than those afforded in family and domestic circles. Unless the French are grossly overrated, they beat the world in politeness. For that sort of polish which qualifies people to glide easily through the forms and requirements of society, they have no equals. Their language lends itself to this accomplishment; and it would seem, too, as though a peculiar suppleness and grace of manner had been given to them for the same end. Nevertheless the French can be decidedly rude when their feelings are touched; and when one remembers how sensitive they 'are, this means that they can often be rude, and that a childish resentment may sometimes be shown, as their own writers admit, where there is no excuse for it. One thing about the French impresses us very oddly, and that is their habit of kissing each other. We mean, of course, kissing between men. The other form is neither French nor Continental—only human. But as to kissing in France, one has to remember that this country, where men are so effusively sentimental as to gush in this manner over their fellow-men, is also the country where the duel finds a congenial home, and where the same persons who saluted but yesterday on bearded cheeks, may salute to-day with clashing swords and eyes aflame with hatred.

That there is a great contrast between city life and country life will readily be believed. This is true in every nation, though, for obvious reasons, it is especially true in France. There is only one Paris, and whatever its excellences or failures otherwise, all will agree that for gayety, for wine and song and dance, and for all the other arts and diversions which by the worldly-minded are thought necessary to drive dull care away and to kill time pleasantly, this city by the Seine has no rival in Europe or America. But from Parisian boulevards to the quaint, sleepy hamlets of France, what a change! You can find rural nooks where even the Parisian language would not be understood; and as to Parisian habits and manners, it is a happy fact in some respects, that rural life as a whole is as different from Paris life as one could either desire or imagine. If the best authorities are to be credited, country life in France is as much distinguished for dullness as city life is for gayety. It is said, too, that in the former of these categories must be classed the sort of life to which Frenchmen are accustomed in the general average of their good-sized towns.

Returning again to a subject of commanding attractiveness, it is the boast of Frenchmen that they are devoted admirers of the fair sex. Woman is their idol, they tell us. We quote only that which is common in both their conversation and their literature when we say that, as regards the generality of Frenchmen, "it is a case of woman-worship." If, however, we admit this, and then look around for the evidences of such worship, how many things we see which stagger us! If the French are true worshipers of woman, how strange it seems that everywhere in the lower classes she is an equal participant with the male species in the drudgery of daily toil! Why is it, too, that French law makes the wife a sharer with the husband in the expenses of family life, and that French custom drags her so often into an active partnership with him in store and market? One would think, too, that a nation of woman-worshipers would make laws for the protection of women against the treachery and baseness of men. Instead of this, however, we find that a betrayed girl in France is not allowed even the poor solace of an action in court against her seducer, and has no claim upon him for the support of her dishonored offspring. What this means in a country reporting 73,936 cases of illegitimacy for 1891, the reader may imagine for himself. We only note these facts as affording another instance of the wide discrepancy one sometimes finds between French sentiment and French practice.

Extending our observations to the department of politics, we still find extremes meeting and contrasts of various kinds obtruding upon our notice. But within this realm greater charity is demanded. France is trying an experiment in her political life. She is on a comparatively new tack; whereas socially and religiously she is the finished product of a thousand years of steady evolution. In the latter aspect she challenges criticism; in the former department she appeals for sympathy. It is not at all strange that we should find in France, side by side with the triumphant champions of democracy, a set of people animated by pride of birth and warmly attached to monarchical institutions. Perhaps, moreover, one of these classes is as reasonably excusable for its love of the old forms as the other is presumptively right in its maintenance of the new. In any case, class antagonism of this sort is only what we might expect, considering that it is yet but twenty years since the Republic experienced its third resurrection. Pity it is, though, that the real aristocracy should have so many shoddy imitators—that so many Frenchmen as they get rich, finding no king to ennoble them, should, as Mr. Hamerton says, "feel justified in ennobling themselves," and should be so silly as to think that by putting the *de* before their names they blossom at once into a set of beings for whom a republican government is not good enough!

We could also wish that the French, having committed themselves to republicanism, were less fond of decorations than they are. The red ribbon of the Legion of Honor is as common on Parisian thoroughfares as gashed cheeks are in Berlin, and is given away, one would think, with almost as free a hand as degrees are lavished upon American clergymen.

As a practical illustration of what France can afford us in the way of political contrasts, we note two recent occurrences in the French capital. One was the decree of the Municipal Council of Paris condemning to destruction the unique-looking "Chapelle Expiatoire," on Boulevard Hausmann, erected by Louis XVIII to the memory of Louis XVI and Marie Antoinette; and the other was when, a few weeks later, upon the centennial anniversary of Louis XVI, most of the Churches of Paris held services and were draped in mourning in his honor, the service at the fashionable Church of Saint François Xavier being attended, as the papers told us, by "the entire aristocracy of Faubourg Saint Germain," and by many representatives of French royalty. Here was a contrast indeed, and perhaps there is food for reflection in it.

Among all the nations, where shall we find one more wedded than the French to the love of glory, or a people more given than these formerly were to the worship of great names? It would seem, though, as if all the heroes of France were now dead. Certainly there is no living greatness which commands worship, or even permanent respect. Popularity in these days is the sure precursor of destruction. Here again do we see the variance which exists between French sentiment and French practice. The national heart pants for great leaders; but French jealousy, like the unkindly frosts of spring, seems destined to blight the budding sprouts of genius before they have time to ripen. This tendency is as distinctly recognized by thoughtful Frenchmen as by students from the outside, and we do not wonder that they see awful possibilities of mischief in it.

Spite of the publicity which they give, on church and school and town hall and everywhere else, to their national motto, the French are far from enjoying to the full either "Liberty, Equality, or Fraternity." There is less liberty for the individual in France than in England. As to equality, there is a better chance in France than in England to acquire property, and particularly land. Perhaps, too, Frenchmen are more nearly equal than Englishmen before the law and in the enjoyment of political rights; but social equality is no more to be looked for in one country than in the other; and in regard to fraternity, a nation which is ceasing to believe in the Fatherhood of God can hardly be expected to illustrate in any marked degree what is meant by the brotherhood of man. Here, then, is another contrast; but we forbear to dwell upon it, for, after all, the people of France, in their political aspirations and in the bold experiment of self-government they are making, deserve charity and commendation far more than censure, or even friendly criticism, and it is quite certain that their greatest dangers lie, not in this department, but within social and moral realms.

MASSES AND CLASSES:
A Study of Industrial Conditions in England.

By REV. HENRY TUCKLEY.

12mo. Cloth. 179 pages. Post-paid, ... 90 cents.

"It describes, with a brotherly pen, the wants, hardships, aspirations, hopes, and present achievements of men and women whose position as wage-earners is similar to that of great multitudes amongst ourselves, but whose opportunities and rewards have been hitherto decidedly inferior to our own."—EXTRACT FROM INTRODUCTION.

OPINIONS OF THE PRESS.

"The book is unassuming in style, but gives in a readable way the observations of a man who has mingled a good deal with the people he studies, and kept his eyes open."—*Springfield (Mass.) Republican.*

This work is devoted to the English bread-winners, the toilers by the Thames, the street-drivers, clerks, shop-assistants, London working-girls, and others. The author says that these English bread-winners are our own kindred, and argues that we should be informed of their situation and needs."—*Scientific American.*

"The style of the book is more popular than scientific, but its facts are just those which workingmen in this country should know and ponder over. In the facts presented, . . . and in the comments made with full recognition of England's social conditions, the author has made a useful volume."—*Boston (Mass.) Journal.*

"The author is a keen observer, and knows well how to present his observations in a clear and orderly way to the reader. The book will be highly prized by all interested in the labor questions in this country. It gives a large body of facts in an accessible form, and a complete picture of industrial England."—*Zion's Herald.*

CRANSTON & CURTS, Cincinnati, Chicago, St. Louis.

BEAUTIFUL PICTURES OF ENGLISH LIFE.

UNDER THE QUEEN; Or, Present-day Life in England.

BY REV. HENRY TUCKLEY.

12mo. Cloth. 278 pages. 90 cents.

"With all her stately buildings, her wealth of history, her stores of learning, her treasures of art, and her many localities of world-wide beauty and renown, there is still nothing in Old England so deeply interesting to the American public as her people."—AUTHOR'S INTRODUCTION.

OPINIONS OF THE PRESS.

From Public Opinion, Washington, D. C.

It is not a book of travel, or the description of public buildings or scenery, but a comparison of the way in which the average Englishman lives with the average American citizen's life. Philanthropists and reformers will find in it much of interest and value. It is a good book to be read by every one who thinks, votes, and tries to help humanity.

From the Inter-Ocean, Chicago.

Mr. Tuckley has a clear and graceful style, and has the faculty of getting hold of facts and circumstances in which the public is sure to be interested. His letters from London covered topics far removed from the beaten track of European correspondents, the intellectual treatment of which called for painstaking research and conscientious fair-mindedness.

Cincinnati Times-Star.

In running over the pages of Mr. Tuckley's book, the opinion grows that it is one of the best descriptions published of late concerning the English people of the present-day, and those who read it will have a thorough comprehension of our British cousins as they are.

From the Transcript, Lexington, Ky.

One of the most charming books of the year. Heretofore writers on England have devoted nearly all their talent to descriptions of historic places, and there is a sameness about these descriptions that is only equaled by their insipidity. But Mr. Tuckley has told us that which we want to know of that country and its people. He has made a great hit in the production of this book.

Two Splendid Books for Young People.

BY THE SAME AUTHOR.

LIFE'S GOLDEN MORNING: Its Promises and its Perils.

12mo. Cloth. 339 pages. 90 cents.

FORWARD MARCH. Talks to Young People on Life and Success.

12mo. Cloth. 239 pages. 90 cents.

CRANSTON & CURTS, PUBLISHERS,
CINCINNATI, CHICAGO, ST. LOUIS.

www.ingramcontent.com/pod-product-compliance
Lightning Source LLC
Chambersburg PA
CBHW031731230426
43669CB00007B/322